David L. Edwards is the author of many books which have been well received. 'Here once again is that marvellous fluency and lucidity, that ability to present complex and conflicting facts and situations completely fairly, those magisterial judgements which combine penetrating insight and down-to-earth common sense, and with it all a sheer readability' (*Church Times*). 'He seems to tackle each subject as it arises as though he had spent half his life studying it and the other half perfecting a way in which to write about it, which is always lucid, invariably balanced and never boring' (*Contemporary Review*). 'He writes comprehensively as well as ecumenically, readably as well as with accurate scholarship' (*Catholic Herald*). 'I stand back in admiration of a man who, if the world could be saved by books alone, would already have saved the world six times over' (*Methodist Recorder*).

Now retired as Provost Emeritus of Southwark Cathedral in London, he was formerly a Fellow of All Souls College, Oxford, Dean of King's College, Cambridge, Sub-Dean of Westminster and Dean of Norwich. He has served the ecumenical movement as Editor of the SCM Press and Chairman of Christian Aid. While at Westminster Abbey he was the Speaker's Chaplain in the House of Commons.

A Concise History
of English Christianity

From Roman Britain to the Present Day

DAVID L. EDWARDS

Fount
An Imprint of HarperCollinsPublishers

Fount Paperbacks in an Imprint of
HarperCollins*Religious*
Part of HarperCollins*Publishers*
77–85 Fulham Palace Road, London W6 8JB

First published in Great Britain
in 1998 by Fount Paperbacks

1 3 5 7 9 10 8 6 4 2

The extracts from *Little Gidding* (from *Four Quartets*)
by T. S. Eliot on pp viii-ix are taken from
Collected Poems 1909–1962, and appear
by kind permission of Faber and Faber Ltd.

A catalogue record for this book is
available from the British Library

Map by John Gilkes

ISBN 0 00 627839 6

Printed and bound in Great Britain by
Caledonian International Book Manufacturing Ltd, Glasgow

Contents

Preface

I wrote a history of *Christian England* from the beginning to 1914 in three volumes, first published 1981–84. A revised edition in one volume appeared in 1989 and was about 1,250 pages in length, although obviously a mere outline of a very long story. I tried to include some account of the nation's official religion and of objections to it; of kings and bishops and of 'ordinary' women and men; of theologians and of poets. The narrative was (I claim) objective and ecumenical and despite its defects it was 'the only modern attempt to tell the history of religion in England within one volume', as was said at the beginning of the useful list of recent studies attached to *A History of Religion in Britain*, a collection of scholarly essays edited by Sheridan Gilley and W. J. Sheils (Blackwell, 1994).

My three volumes remain available in libraries, I hope, but I have been asked to sum up the story even more concisely, reconsidering everything in it, continuing it to 1997, and offering some brief reflections about its significance now that fourteen hundred years have passed since the missionaries from Rome approached the Anglo-Saxons. And I was asked to keep in mind the background in the history of Christianity elsewhere in the world, an immense subject which I tried to survey in *Christianity: The First Two Thousand Years* (1997). I have been glad to do what I could to respond to this challenge, hoping that this new book will reach people who have no time to go into the details of history. I shall be additionally glad if by this service I am able to encourage any reader to move on to the works on which I have myself depended. I should like to repay a little of my debt to the people and places who, across half a century, have taught me as much as the books, in Canterbury, Oxford, Cambridge, Westminster, Norwich and Southwark; and a little of what I owe to the Student Christian Movement and the British Council of Churches for experiences which now mean that although I am happy to be a priest of the Church of England this book is by no means intended as Anglican propaganda.

My aim is that despite its own limitations and defects this introduction will do something to show that the history of English Christianity is a topic worth exploring, whether or not we who live in a very different time are regular churchgoers and whether or not we can agree about who was in the right in the disputes of earlier generations.

T. S. Eliot referred to those disputes in *Little Gidding*:

> We cannot revive old factions
> We cannot restore old policies
> Or follow an antique drum.
> These men, and those who opposed them
> And those whom they opposed,
> Accept the constitution of silence
> And are folded in a single party.

But Eliot also knew that something more needed to be said.

> What the dead had no speech for when living,
> They can tell you, being dead: the communication
> Of the dead is tongued with fire beyond the language of the living.

And so he found 'on a winter's afternoon, in a secluded chapel', that

> We die with the dying:
> See, they depart, and we go with them.

We are born with the dead:
See, they return, and bring us with them.

The short last chapter offers some thoughts about what may develop after AD 2000. Of course it cannot be based on facts as the other chapters have been, but one of the uses of history is to stimulate ideas about what may grow in the future on the basis of knowledge about trends in the past; so my opinions may encourage a reader to form a different estimate of possibilities or to raise a prayer for a better outcome. And at least the inclusion of this unusual chapter may show that this book is not intended to be a textbook which must be studied in preparation for an examination. I enjoyed writing it – may it be found enjoyable to read! Some readers may be unfamiliar with some of the words but I have tried to explain any technical term and to make the index useful.

D.L.E., Winchester, Pentecost 1997

The Vision of William Blake

And did those feet in ancient time
Walk upon England's mountains green?
And was the holy Lamb of God
On England's pleasant pastures seen?

And did the Countenance Divine
Shine forth upon our clouded hills?
And was Jerusalem builded here,
Among these dark Satanic mills?

Bring me my Bow of burning gold:
Bring me my Arrows of desire:
Bring me my Spear: O clouds unfold!
Bring me my Chariot of fire!

I will not cease from Mental Fight,
Nor shall my Sword sleep in my hand:
Till we have built Jerusalem
In England's green & pleasant Land.

A Prologue in Ancient Time

Roman Britain

In the opening years of the nineteenth Christian century William Blake worked on a long poem, *Milton*. The short poem which he put at its beginning became almost an alternative national anthem for the English more than a hundred years later, when set to uplifting music by Parry in order to defy the grimness of the First World War. Blake wrote it as the battle song of a dissenting radical. He prefaced it by the summons 'Rouze up, O Young Men of the New Age', and on the back of his last drawing to go with *Milton* he wrote: 'I return from flame of fire tried & pure & white'. But in the twentieth century this poem, usually called *Jerusalem*, was to owe some of its popularity to the possible interpretation of its mysterious words as a conservative hymn, a lament full of nostalgia for an age of gold or at least of green fields.

The poem was based on the absurd legend that as a boy Jesus was brought to England by Joseph of Arimathea, who appears briefly in the gospels as the rich man who provided the tomb after the crucifixion. Blake dreamed about what might have followed a visit by 'the holy Lamb of God': the building of the ideal City of God, the new Jerusalem, 'in England's green & pleasant Land'. A biblical text which he attached to the poem was used as a summons to all the people of England to be prophets, and although almost always ignored or ridiculed in his lifetime the poet saw himself as resembling the prophet Elijah, ascending to heaven from Ancient Israel on a chariot of fire. At the age of four he had, he believed, seen God pressing his face against the window. As he grew he saw eternity everywhere in life, the divine creativity in all life, the divine suffering in all pain. He worshipped the Jesus who had commanded his disciples to preach 'against Religion and Government'. He could speak and write very simply, and one reason why he buried his message in a mythology which most people found baffling if they troubled to look into it was indicated by a comment he made on a book which offered a conventional defence of the authority of Scripture. Really to defend the Bible, he remarked, would get a man hanged.

For many years the figure of Joseph of Arimathea had fascinated him. He began making engravings to reproduce his drawings while he was an apprentice in London, and the first of these, made at the age of sixteen in 1773, portrayed Joseph brooding on a rock on the English coast. When he re-engraved this picture many years later, he was not content with the legend that Joseph brought to Europe, and according to some accounts to England, the 'holy grail' which was the cup used at the Last Supper. He preferred the story that Joseph and the boy Jesus jointly constructed a church at Glastonbury in Somerset. He now claimed that his picture was of 'one of the Gothic Artists who Built the Cathedrals in what we call the Dark Ages'. In real life the young Blake spent months in Westminster Abbey, drawing the royal tombs and much of the rest of the architecture which was thought to have avoided Roman discipline by being 'Gothic' in its energy. He had a vision of Jesus and his apostles walking through the great church. What gripped his imagination, and his whole life, was an idea formed by these and other early influences: the idea that the original 'religion of Jesus' – to Blake 'Mercy, Pity, Love, Peace' and 'continual forgiveness' – had flourished in the 'ancient time' and could be revived. This was the 'Sublime of the Bible' to which he referred in his preface to *Milton* but it had, he maintained, been corrupted by preachers who terrified their congregations by doctrines about a God of law, wrath and hell. Even England's greatest poets had not proclaimed the ancient, true and revolutionary religion: 'Shakespeare & Milton were both curb'd.' Now Blake felt inspired to arise as a new

Milton, with a trumpet calling a new generation to 'Mental Fight' – a conflict far more important than the long war waged against Revolutionary and Napoleonic France.

He announced part of his message by combining the words 'green' and 'pleasant' at the beginning and the end of this introductory poem. It seems that he wrote it in a cottage in Sussex, but he had lived in the Lambeth district of London for ten years from 1790 and had been acutely sensitive to what he saw around him: a city full of poverty, disease and other misery. To him the beginnings of industrialization had been a lived nightmare. The mention of 'Dark Satanic mills' may have been suggested by the ruins of what had been London's first large factory, the Albion Mill, built a short distance from his house in order to grind flour for London's new population to buy if they could afford it. The ruins seemed to him 'Satanic' because the factory was a symbol of the destruction of the old England, its jobs and its pleasures, by the new machines. The walls were 'dark' because blackened by fire, probably caused by arson.

In this book we shall meet (however briefly) many English people who, like that indignant prophet, have held beliefs and lived lives connected with Jesus Christ – and some who, like Blake, have seen visions and dreamed dreams. That is a massively solid and important part of the history of England although some recent historians appear to have forgotten that between the early years of the eighth century and the closing years of the nineteenth, England could be called a Christian country and could be so called with considerable justice provided that 'Christian' is not taken to mean saintly. This English Christianity has been exported to many parts of the world along with the English language, and has outlasted the British empire which helped it to cross the oceans and the continents. This history, astonishing when we remember how small is the island of 'Great' Britain, has created a considerable number of international denominations, Anglican and Methodist, Baptist and Congregational, along with the Society of Friends, the Salvation Army and other relatively small bodies. Scotland was the first secure homeland of English-speaking Presbyterians, but it was in a chamber adjoining Westminster Abbey in 1646 that the 'Westminster Confession' was drawn up as a standard statement of Presbyterian faith. In the same room the most famous of the English translations of the Bible, the Authorized or King James Version, had been edited 35 years previously. And the fascination which that abbey had for the young Blake may remind us that England was a Catholic country, as devoutly Catholic as any in Europe, for about a thousand years. Its Roman Catholic community has of course survived and grown after the Protestant Reformation: Cardinal Newman rightly celebrated the growth as being like an unpredictable 'second spring' in the year.

All that Christian life makes a story which is worth telling although it is hard to do justice to it, and which deserves attention although it does not always get it. But if the tale is to be told truthfully it cannot be a continuous story of faith and idealism, for the actors in these dramas were human beings who could not avoid being handicapped, and who were often bound to disagree with each other, all the more fiercely because the questions in dispute seemed momentously and eternally important. In this book there will be an attempt to take seriously both what Blake called the 'burning gold' and the realities which we can observe if we are not sentimental; both the 'Chariot of fire' and the mud beneath the chariot's launch into space. For the combination of the saintly and the sordid made history as it was lived.

* * *

It is obvious that in reality the feet of Jesus of Nazareth never walked in the country which began to be called 'Englaland' about a thousand years after his birth. Jesus lived at one end of the Roman empire. This island, then containing more forests than green fields, was at the other end, and Julius Caesar had not thought it worthwhile to pay it more than a brief military expedition, some sixty years before Mary had a son. Yet eventually the Romans did occupy what they called Britannia, beginning about a dozen years after the crucifixion of Jesus by another part of their army. It is also a fact that the feet of Christians – the new people called by St Paul 'the Body of Christ' – first walked in Roman Britain three hundred (or more) years before missionaries arrived to convert the island's Anglo-Saxon invaders. But if we are looking for the truth about that ancient time we shall have to consider the evidence provided by a few stones which archaeologists have unearthed (and debated in arguments about their significance), supplemented by a few sentences (often also of uncertain significance) written when the Roman army had left. Not a single letter or other document written in Britain under Roman occupation has survived: we must blame the damp climate.

We do not know who first brought Christianity to Britannia, some time after the invasion in the year which was to be called *Anno Domini* ('in the year of the Lord') 43. In 61 the temple in Colchester, recently built in honour of the emperor who had ordered this invasion, Claudius, was burned down by British resistance fighters led by a queen remembered in the English tradition as Boadicea. These warriors were members of a tribe belonging to the widely spread Celtic race and they were encouraged in battle by their priests, the *druides*. The Romans crushed the rebel army and dealt with the turbulent priests. They did not attempt to suppress the religion of the natives, however. It was always their policy to tolerate, and even to encourage, the worship of gods and goddesses who could be amalgamated with their own divinities as the contented patrons of a contented empire. To give only one example, a new temple in the style of the Greeks and Romans was built at Lydney in Gloucestershire in the fourth Christian century, and dedicated to the Celtic god Noden who was identified with the Roman god Mars. A guest house was attached for people who came in search of healing. Possibly another temple in Gloucestershire, at Uley, was converted into a church, for a Christian casket had been found on the site, but like much else about Roman Britain this is uncertain: the casket may have been offered to Mercury, who was worshipped there.

The evidence suggests that the Church was a minority – a very small minority until the emperors Constantine and Theodosius made Christianity the empire's official religion during the fourth century. This Church's first martyr, Albanus, seems to have been executed in about 210. A rich shrine commemorating him developed in Verulamium, which became known as St Albans. The names of two other martyrs, Julius and Aaron, have been preserved: the name of the latter is a reminder that the religion about Jesus of Nazareth was spread first among the Jews, who were dispersed all over the Roman empire, a vast area dominated by the memory of Julius Caesar. Writing some two hundred years after Christ's birth, Tertullian of Carthage boasted that parts of Britain beyond the reach of Rome had been conquered by him. If there was any substance in that claim by a rhetorical Christian who lived far away, it must have referred to some Christian presence in the south-west of Britain, which the imperial army was slow to control but which did have trading links with Gaul (the term used to refer to France before it was conquered by the Franks in the sixth Christian century). In 314 three British bishops went to a council at Arles in the south of Gaul, from London, York and Lincoln, accompanied by a priest and a deacon. They travelled safely at a time when the emperor Constantine had just emerged as a Christian. He had begun his war against his rivals for the throne when proclaimed emperor in the military headquarters in York, the site on which York Minster was to be built. In 359 three other British bishops were paid their expenses by the government when they attended a similar council at Rimini in Italy, but it was reported that this time other bishops who went from Britain said that they could afford to be self-supporting.

Before this astonishing transformation of the Church's position in the empire, Christianity had been half-hidden. The first words on the Lord's Prayer in Latin could be scratched on plaster, but the letters of *Pater noster* were mixed with others which would baffle a mere passer-by: examples of this cryptogram have been found in Manchester and Cirencester. After the change under Constantine, well-to-do Christians could openly include Christian symbols in the art for which they paid. At Lullingstone in Kent part of a villa (a substantial farmhouse) was set aside as a church; on the walls six Christians, perhaps members of the family which owned the villa, were portrayed standing in prayer with arms upraised, as was then the custom. At Hinton St Mary in Dorset a mosaic pavement in another villa depicted scenes of hunting but had at its centre a fairly crude little portrait of a clean-shaven Christ; around his face are the Greek letters *chi* and *rho*, the letters which Constantine had told his soldiers to paint on their shields as a sign that Christ was his patron. A number of lead tanks marked by Christian symbols have been unearthed: probably they were fonts used in the baptisms of adult converts to the new religion.

Some of the evidence seems to indicate that the Christians themselves became guilty of violence and persecution. In London the temple of Mithras (originally a Persian god) seems to have been popular with soldiers and other men who adorned it with marble statues, but in the early 300s it was attacked and closed. It seems probable that the violence came from Christians who did not fear punishment if they forcibly closed down a centre of pagan worship, and it is not at all unlikely that later in that century Christians hoped that all such temples would be closed down permanently now that the Roman empire was becoming Christian. But if so, hopes of ages of triumphant peace were short lived. In the middle of the fourth century valuable items of silver and gold were buried at Mildenhall in Suffolk and at Water Newton near Peterborough (and no doubt also elsewhere). Christian symbols were on some of these pieces, and the Water Newton hoard seems to have belonged to a church because it included plaques which had been fixed to walls, as was the custom in pagan temples. This treasure was hidden in a time of panic about raids from the north and the east – and was never recovered, presumably because the owners fled or were killed. Another treasure, discovered at Thetford in Norfolk, seems to have been buried in the 390s: it was marked with the name of a pagan god. In may have been buried in order to save it from Christians or because the times were dangerous for Christians and pagans alike. Soon various warrior-bands of Angles, Saxons, Jutes and other Germanic tribesmen arrived, either as mercenaries hired to replace the Roman soldiers or as uninvited settlers. Peace was over.

Early in the 400s Rome left the islanders responsible for their own defence, and soon no new coins were being minted, but there is some evidence about a Church strong enough to outlast this new time of troubles. A copy of a short and simple book about the Christian life written for the benefit of a widow called Fatalis by a British bishop called Fastidius in about 425 survives in an Italian monastery. An account written in about 480 survives of a visit by two bishops from Gaul to the martyr Alban's shrine in 429. They preached against the doctrines of Pelagius, a theologian born in Britain probably in about

360. While teaching in Rome (where he had studied) he was believed to have stressed the freedom and importance of the human will at the expense of a proper emphasis on God's initiatives; the Pelagians who defended these doctrines were said to be rich, dressed in 'dazzling robes' and 'surrounded by an adoring crowd'. The visitors are said to have won the argument by performing a miracle. There is also a report that the bishops persuaded a British army to be baptized before winning a battle.

Considerable numbers of pagan Anglo-Saxons arrived in Britain from the 450s onwards but in this period British Christianity developed the characteristics known as Celtic; or it did so at least in areas which the invaders did not reach. Latin was still used in worship and there were still bishops, but monasteries were now becoming the centres of church life: they had originated in Egypt in the fourth century and their example of praying and working in a disciplined community had spread to Western Europe through Gaul. Roman Britain had been organized in districts called *civitates*; on the roads, milestones showed the distance to the nearest main town. Now the towns gradually decayed and were largely deserted. In Silchester near Basingstoke, for example, a building which was probably (not certainly) a church was taken over by squatters in the fifth or sixth century. The villas where Christian landowners had acted as the patrons of rural congregations were no longer secure and they, too, were often abandoned or occupied by squatters. It began to seem sensible that a monastery which offered few attractions to the men of violence looking for loot should replace the town and the villa. Some archaeologists have seen stones as evidence for the foundation of a monastery at Tintagel high on the Cornish cliffs about 500, but most of these Celtic monasteries were far less conspicuous: it was only photography from the air in the 1960s that revealed where they had been, and then only when the photographer took advantage of the shadows in the fields as the sun was about to set.

Celtic Christianity also flourished in the little British kingdom to the north of Wales and in another 'Little Britain', Brittany. We have the name of the leader of the migration of British refugees across the Channel in the fifth century, for a bishop already in Gaul wrote to him, and in 461 Mansuetus, 'bishop of the British', attended a council in Tours. Probably towards the end of the century Ninian, 'a most venerable and holy man', was the British missionary bishop in the south-west of Scotland, based at a stone-and-plaster church in Whithorn, which has been excavated. The tombstone of Latinus and his daughter aged four has survived in this outpost: under their names 'We praise thee, O God' was bravely carved in Latin. The most famous British missionary bishop, however, was Patrick, who before his death in about 460 made an impact on Ireland, to which he had been taken at the age of sixteen as a slave. Two short writings by him survive. In contrast, very little is known for certain about the saintly monks among the British in Wales such as Illtud, who was influential in the sixth century, and David, who long after his death in about 600 became the patron saint of the Welsh. What is known about Celtic Christianity in Wales and Cornwall in about 550 is that a fierce writer, Gildas, denounced it for being scarcely less corrupt than the brutal local rulers. It seems possible that by the time of David's death the indignation of Gildas had been a factor in the renewal of the Church's holiness, with lasting effects. A modern Welsh historian, Glanmor Williams, has summed up the people's religion which endured for many centuries: 'They reposed their trust in the prowess of their saints and in the ritual performed by their clergy to safeguard them from evil and to ensure their salvation in the world to come.'

The Britons who remained in what became England did not give up their land without fighting. A book about a hermit who lived early in the 700s says that he was often troubled by nightmares about the attacks by the Britons which he had experienced while he had been a soldier: this suggests a resistance continuing some 250 years after the first landings of the Anglo-Saxons. According to a mass of stories and songs popular in the Middle Ages, the greatest hero of this resistance was Arthur, and it seems possible that this hero did not belong entirely to the world of the imagination. Arthur was not mentioned by Gildas who, however, clearly wrote in a time of peace, on which he blamed the decadence: Arthur may have secured that peace. A Welsh poem written about 600 celebrates a military hero 'although he was not Arthur'. More than two hundred years later it was recorded that

Arthur had been the 'leader of the battles' who had won twelve great victories. In the second half of the tenth century a Welsh chronicler wrote concerning the year 518: 'In the battle of Badon Arthur carried the cross of our Lord Jesus Christ on his shoulders for three days and the Britons were the victors.' According to this source, Arthur was killed in another battle, in 539. Unfortunately there must be doubts about the historical value of these traditions and archaeology has not supplied any information.

What do these fragments of evidence signify? The gods and goddesses of the pagan Celts seem to have been the personifications of natural forces. Thunder was alarming, water gushed out of the earth, people were intoxicated by alcohol or love, babies were born, crops grew from seeds, battles were won – and those who marvelled worshipped. They worshipped with fear: the Romans, who were far from squeamish, were shocked by the druids' practice of human sacrifice to appease the gods. But the more 'civilized' (because more city-based) religion of the Romans also had origins in the worship of wonderful power, including the power of the Roman emperors, who were treated as divine. Into this paganism, Celtic or Roman, came the Christian religion which claimed that God is one and that God is love. The Roman empire was hostile to it, mainly because Christians hoped for the 'Kingdom of God' with Jesus as king: that did not sound like loyalty to the empire. The strange new religion inherited the Jewish belief in God as supernaturally holy and as the Creator of all: it proclaimed a definite creed and could defend it by argument. It also taught a definite morality and could recommend it as a practical possibility, as when Bishop Fastidius encouraged Fatalis in about 425 to try to imitate Christ, to be modestly contented despite her bereavement, and to be busy with good works. It honoured martyrs and monks and in Pelagius it produced a theologian who maintained that many could become saints if they had the will.

Thus the new religion, at first unpopular precisely because it was unique, had a strength which made Constantine pick it out as a good ally in his campaign to reconstruct the Roman empire, with himself as the sole and sacred emperor. In the future the Church on this island, as in every other country in Europe, was to depend greatly on support by governments, and was to accept control by them as the price to be paid for this support; but the future was also to show that the ability of the Christians to survive in Britain after the end of Roman colonialism was not the last example of this religion's ability to renew itself in hard times and to stand in its own strength. If we ask what was the nature of this strength, and if we are to be honest, we have to admit that Christians have disagreed – often furiously – about the right answer. But some thoughts are suggested by the fragmentary evidence about the origins of Christianity in Britannia.

In the future, Christians were to create many masterpieces of architecture, 'to the glory of God', and in every village there was to be at least one church as the community's heart. But few separate buildings which were probably churches in Roman Britain had been excavated by the last years of the twentieth century, and those which have been unearthed were not large. This suggests that before any impressive church was built the Church was present as a group of people. In most of the religious practices of the pre-Christian Roman empire the people admired a temple but did not enter it. They brought animals to it, which priests acting on their behalf sacrificed. For Christianity what mattered most was that the people should themselves be a 'royal priesthood' offering the spiritual sacrifice of consecrated lives: that construction of a new humanity was the building of the true 'temple of God'. And often to its own surprise, in the centuries to come the Church was to discover, and to rediscover, that it did not entirely depend on any particular building, or on any particular furniture.

In the future, the buildings of the Church, when popular, were to be the scenes of practices which could be attacked as pagan or magical because they recited prayers for miracles convenient for those offering the prayers, and often these prayers were to be made before statues not totally unlike the images of the old pagan gods and goddesses. Whether or not this Protestant attack on popular Catholicism was fair is a question which can be disputed, while it is certain that a spiritual life which has been genuinely Christian has been encouraged by Catholic faith. But if we look at the origins of Christianity in Britain we see that its appeal cannot have depended mainly on anything which was more or less identical with what was offered by paganism, for the country had already had prestigious divinities, Celtic or Roman, to whom petitions could be addressed. What Christianity offered was a new morality, as Blake insisted, with all the emphasis on love, and often in this history we shall notice that the real religion of most of the English was largely moral rather than dogmatic. But the supremacy of love has always needed justification in a harsh world, and the image central to Christianity has been so scandalous that so far as we know the early Christians did not care to produce a devotional picture or sculpture of it: the supremacy of love has been asserted by the shattering image of God the Son dying on a cross. Yet somehow the story of Jesus of Nazareth, 'Christ crucified', made converts, even in the Roman army. In the centuries to come there were to be refinements which made it psychologically possible for crucifixes to be painted and carved. It was to be taught that God the Father did not suffer, nor did the divine nature of God the Son, and that the human nature of the Son suffered only in order that a sacrifice might be offered on behalf of human sinners. But it was to be possible for Blake to express a simple thought:

> He doth give His joy to all,
> He becomes an infant small.
> He becomes a man of woe,
> He doth feel the sorrow too ...
>
> O! He gives to us His joy
> That our grief He may destroy;
> Till our grief is fled and gone
> He doth sit by us and moan.

The prayer which was the Lord's and therefore the Church's was scratched on plaster in the years under persecution. It was addressed to the one eternal Creator, and it dared to call him 'Our Father'. The image of Christ in a mosaic floor could be accompanied by other images (the Hinton St Mary floor depicted hunting as the favourite sport and also illustrated pagan mythology), but Christ was not merely one decorative image among many. He was worshipped, and in the Lullingstone villa Christians prayed through him to the heavenly Father. Baptism meant standing naked while water was being poured over the head into a river or a tank: it was a symbol of sharing the very cold water of Christ's death before rising to live with him in glory for ever. As worship was given to Christ as God the Son, it was to become unthinkable that his image should be part of a floor and so liable to be trodden upon. And what modern archaeologists have never found in any excavation is very revealing. They have uncovered sites which were probably Christian cemeteries (and one, at Pound-bury near Dorchester in Dorset, which was certainly that) but have never found that 'grave goods' were buried with the bodies of Christians. It was believed that in heaven, 'with Christ', there would be not need of pots made of earth or jewels made of heated metal and pretty stones.

The new faith came from the Mediterranean and must have been spread in Britannia by Christians who traded with this northern extension of the Roman empire or who were refugees from persecution in Gaul. The story told about the martyr Alban was that he was a Roman soldier who had been converted by the quiet holiness of a Christian priest he had sheltered. That priest, the story said, came from Gaul. The first evidence about British bishops comes from their attendance at a council in Gaul. The account of the visit to Alban's shrine by bishops from Gaul many years later is probably not sober history, but the story indicates that the British Church was still regarded as inferior to the Church in Gaul. As the tale goes, Britain's Christians included leaders who were well dressed and a crowd of people interested in a theological argument, but at the end of the debate they accepted the doctrine which the Church in Gaul believed, and the story that there was a need to baptize the British army suggests that more than a hundred years after Constantine's triumph, membership of the Church was limited. It is all the more remarkable that the British Church, so far from the Mediterranean, was able to survive and develop, at least in the west of the island, when it was cut off from Gaul. For these British Christians whose early predecessors had endured the Roman empire's persecution now had to face conquest by the Anglo-Saxon pagans.

An Anglo-Saxon poem called *The Ruin* has been preserved in the library of Exeter Cathedral. It seems to describe the decay of the temple in Bath which had been dedicated to the Celtic goddess Sulis, identified with the Romans' Minerva. The poet meditated gloomily on the fate of buildings which seemed to have been built by giants. Broken tiles had fallen from the roof to the ground, and rain-soaked walls were covered with lichen. People had been proud and merry here, flushed with wine, glittering in their armour or splashing in the warm springs: now they were buried beneath the rubble on the frozen ground. It is a vivid picture of the collapse of the whole civilization of Rome. But it is not a complete picture of Britain in these 'dark ages', for whether or not they were led to glorious victories by a real Arthur in real history it is clear that the British or Celtic Christians did not entirely share the gloom which is the mood of much Anglo-Saxon poetry (not solely of *The Ruin*). They took the Gospel and built the Church, changing the history of Wales and Cornwall, Scotland and Ireland. Their successors founded impressive monasteries in Gaul and Italy and, pursuing the self-discipline of 'pilgrimage for the love of God', took their tiny boats into the Atlantic, reaching land. They did all this because of the intensity and hopefulness of their Christian faith, although no doubt their religion was often valued by the new Christians as a superior kind of magic.

The evidence which has survived about this faith suggests that it both lost and gained because it had developed outside the influence of the Roman genius for law and order. It established itself in the west of Britannia when the great empire was declining and falling, and the Romans never got as far as Ireland. The organization, or lack of it, in the Celtic Church therefore proved vulnerable when a Catholicism based on Rome arrived in force but for the time being it could fit into the surrounding tribal society. Its bishops and other leaders were usually sons of local chiefs or aristocrats, and the local clergy were usually married, but the Church's spiritual life was not based on the Roman arrangement of an area round a city with its resident bishop. What mattered was the monastery where unmarried monks could carry on a fervent life of worship and self-denial without too much influence by the local chief or by the more-or-less barbaric customs of the society. The head of an important monastery, an 'abbot', would not need to take orders from any bishop. These monks were, however, not cut off from the tribe around them: they went out as pastors and evangelists and there could be an adjacent religious community of women under the same abbot. Such church life did not require much expenditure or administration, and instead of needing to extract gifts from the local chiefs by flattery, bishops and priests could frighten them by being strangely austere. They took sin very seriously, as is shown by their 'penitentials' which prescribed how sorrow for sin should be expressed by long periods of harsh self-discipline, but they united this insistence on holiness as the Christian goal with a realistic understanding of the steps to be taken on the way. Their intimate talks with 'soul friends' (usually monks but not necessarily priests) were the origin of the practice of confessing sins privately to a priest and receiving spiritual direction: a practice which became centrally important in Catholicism. The spirituality of this Church combined a contempt for soft comforts with a great respect for the Bible and for some other books; a refusal to worship the forces of nature with a delight in the beauties of God's creation; the orthodoxy of the Latin Mass with an informal holiness in every-day prayers. The conquest of demons by Christ the 'High King of Heaven' seemed a reality vivid because fresh: this Christianity had only recently defeated paganism. Such a religion, free from any dependence on the Roman empire, could be close to the earth and to the poor, and it made some tough saints who were believed to have an uncanny power even after death.

How far did this British or Celtic Christianity, which is known to have been strong elsewhere, influence those parts of the country which the pagan Anglo-Saxons occupied? It is a question discussed by modern scholars but no evidence can supply a clear answer. Twenty place names preserved by the Anglo-Saxons suggest the presence of a British church, an *ecles* (derived from the Latin *ecclesia*), but any church in such a village was a small wooden structure, perhaps a shed, which has disappeared. In Glastonbury a larger church made of timber was revered as ancient when it was reached by the West Saxons under their king Ine, who died in 722. It was not the Gothic cathedral imagined by Blake, and it had not been built by an apprentice carpenter from Israel called Jesus, but Ine the conqueror gave lands to support its clergy and the building continued to be revered until it was destroyed by fire in 1184.

Other evidence is even more uncertain. We have no report about any British bishop or priest at work in the area which the Anglo-Saxons occupied before the eighth century. It seems possible that the mass baptisms which were to respond to the new missionaries who came from abroad were influenced not only by the example or orders given by the local chief but also by memories, however dim, of British Christianity. But there is also no report that the missionaries were welcomed by British Christians who had already been baptized. There may well have been such Christians, for in an emergency there can be a valid baptism without a priest, but if so they kept very quiet according to the evidence that has survived.

What is clear is that at the end of the sixth Christian century missionaries treated England as a pagan country. They assumed that there had to be a new start.

2

Mountains

Anglo-Saxon England, 597–1066

There were some peak moments in the history of Anglo-Saxon Christianity. One came in 597, when Augustine led forty other monks sent from Rome to convert Ethelbert, King of Kent. Bede, the usually careful historian to whom we owe most of our knowledge of this period, gathered information about local traditions and was supplied with evidence preserved in Rome. According to his account, the missionaries chanted in Latin as they walked behind a silver cross and an icon (a painted image) of Jesus. The king had insisted on a first meeting in the open air, fearing magic, and what was advancing to meet him was indeed magic in at least one sense: these monks were ambassadors of a society which spoke the language of civilization, had technical skills and proclaimed a saviour with an assurance which impressed pagan tribesmen. Ethelbert had, however, met Christians before: indeed he had been married to one, Bertha, for at least ten years. She was the daughter of the Frankish king who ruled the Paris region, and had brought a chaplain with her. He was a bishop who may have gathered a Christian community around him already, but there is no record of that. The marriage was only one of many contacts between Kent and Gaul: the graves of landowners in Kent contained imported jewels, weapons, cups and wine. With this pressure in the background, soon Ethelbert was baptized. He allowed the missionaries to use the little Roman church which was already the queen's chapel. Later on Augustine set up his headquarters in another church which had been abandoned but now became the first Canterbury Cathedral; a small part of it has been rediscovered by archaeology. A sixth-century copy of the gospels which was almost certainly sent from Rome for the missionaries' use is still preserved in Cambridge. Thus Catholic worship was resumed in a Roman city which was largely in ruins.

This mission did not come from the part of Britannia inhabited by the Welsh, a name derived from the Anglo-Saxons for 'foreigners'. Bede, normally a gentle scholar reading, writing and teaching in his Northumbrian monastery in Jarrow, found it impossible to forgive the Welsh for their failure to share their faith with the English. He recorded with relish the 'very great slaughter' of Welsh monks who had been praying to 'their God' during one battle. Some personal names hint that relations between the two races were not always hostile: Celtic names were given to early members of the royal house of Wessex, presumably by their mothers. Some place names always used by the Anglo-Saxons originated in the names of Celtic tribes: Cumberland, for example, or Kent. But most contacts seem to have been cold if not violent. Bede preserved the story that when British bishops from the west went to meet Augustine he showed his contempt by refusing to rise to greet them. A consequence was that they refused to be impressed when he announced that he was carrying instructions from Rome. Bede mentioned seven bishops and other 'teachers' meeting Augustine from 'the neighbouring province of the Britons'.

The mission had been sent to England by Pope Gregory the Great, who believed that the world was about to come to an end but that nevertheless he had a duty to convert pagans on this island on the known world's edge. Early in the 700s a biographer told the story of how Gregory had admired some young Angles as 'angels' because these slaves on sale in Rome were sturdy, handsome and fair-haired, and it is a fact that in 595 he had ordered a priest who was his agent in Gaul to buy some English youths in the slave market, in order that they might be turned into monks in Rome and trained to be missionaries among their own people. We also know from his surviving letters that he took the trouble to instruct and encourage Augustine, who needed to be urged forward in a mission which was not without its dangers.

Some of Gregory's ideas did not prove practical: he wanted Augustine to establish two new provinces of the Catholic Church, each with twelve bishops. Their archbishops were to be based on London and York, names remembered from the days of the Roman empire. That was a dream. But some of his orders could be carried out. Having first ordered the destruction of all objects connected with paganism, he later thought it a better idea to convert pagan temples and festivals to Christian uses. The give-and-take relationship between Christianity and England had begun.

Initially everything depended on support by the kings, who were chiefs of the tribes into which the Anglo-Saxons were still divided. If they welcomed the missionaries, others did and were baptized in considerable numbers; if not, not. These petty kings were often at war with each other but they could be attracted to Christianity, partly because it had the prestige of being the dominant religion in England's slightly more civilized neighbour, Gaul, where the Frankish king Clovis had been baptized together with much of his army. Ethelbert was the strongest chief in what had been Britannia, the *bretwalda*, followed in that precarious position by Redwald the king of the East Saxons, and then by Edwin the king of the Angles to the north of the river Humber. The missionaries were no doubt delighted to receive a backing from such rulers, and the very first clause of Ethelbert's code of laws for Kent (the first written code in English) threatened severe penalties for anyone stealing the property of churchmen. But Bede says that pagan temples functioned in Kent until the 640s.

In East Anglia Redwald was only half persuaded: he placed a Christian altar in his chapel without removing the temple's pagan contents, and Bede draws attention to the fact that his queen remained a firm pagan. Probably this was the king in whose honour the treasure now on view in the British Museum was buried in Sutton Hoo. The treasure is ambiguous in what little it says about religion: the whole burial, in a rowing boat which had presumably been used as a royal barge, looks definitely pagan, yet no trace of a body has been found and it seems just possible that the king was given a Christian burial elsewhere. Two silver spoons, perhaps given to Redwald by Ethelbert, have on their handles the names SAULOS and PAULOS, a reminder of the more thorough convert to Christianity who became St Paul. The Northumbrian king Edwin married a daughter of Ethelbert and allowed her to bring a Christian chaplain to his court, Paulinus. This missionary baptized the king and others, including a man who later recalled to a priest (who told Bede) what the stranger had looked like: 'tall, a little stooping, with black hair, a thin face and a slender, hooked nose'. But in the north as in the south there were setbacks.

When he came to the throne Ethelbert's son showed forcibly that he had remained a pagan. There was a period when it seemed that the mission to Kent would have to be abandoned, until the new king agreed to marry another princess from Gaul and also to embrace her Christian faith. Sigbert, king of the East Angles, became a Christian while in exile in Gaul, and on his return was the patron of Felix, a bishop from Burgundy who founded the Church in East Anglia, but he was eventually murdered by the pagan warriors around him: they complained that he forgave his enemies too easily. The slowness of the conversion of the East Saxons made it impossible to establish London as the Christian headquarters. And although in Northumbria Edwin remained a Christian, when this king had been killed in battle Bishop Paulinus had to flee and 'James the deacon' was left alone to carry on the mission to the north.

Bede's history reads like a tale of success for Christian evangelism, without any story of a martyrdom, but a closer look at the evidence does not support any idea that the conversion of the Anglo-Saxons was quick or easy. Bede includes a story which allows us to see that people who had been compelled to accept the destruction of their old religion as ordered by their kings could still be hostile to the new Church: a crowd on the banks of the river Tyne jeered as some monks clumsily handling small boats were in danger of being swept out to sea. A year before his death Bede sent a letter to a former pupil who was now a bishop, complaining that many villages never saw a priest, that many peasants were still unable to recite the Lord's Prayer, and that landowners had founded monasteries merely in order to reduce the assets which could be used by the king in war.

The churches built in this period were small even when they were not made of wood. One was built at Bradwell-on-Sea in Essex using bricks taken from the Roman fort at Othona: it is still used for Christian worship but can never have held many worshippers. Bishop Wilfred led the mission to the South Saxons when in the 680s (no earlier) his ship was driven by a storm to the coast of Sussex. He worked mainly in the north, and the crypts (basements) of the churches he built in Ripon and Hexham survive: they, too, are small. Many stone crosses survive in the countryside and it is believed that they mark places where Christian worship was held in the open air before any church was built, although they may also have marked the graves of prominent Christians. It was only in the eighth century that pagan burials ceased.

The results which were achieved were mixed, with the continuation of many pagan customs and images. The Franks Casket now in the British Museum is a piece of a whale's bone carved with scenes from the Bible and from pagan mythology. Easter is still named after the Anglo-Saxon goddess Eostre, and the days of the week in English commemorate not only worship of the sun and the moon but also the divinities Tiw, Woden, Thor and Frigg. Some two hundred years after Augustine's arrival inspectors of the English Church reported to Rome that many of the people still worshipped the old gods on hilltops, and wore pagan charms. From the same period complaints survive that even bishops, monks and nuns kept up the Anglo-Saxon habit of getting drunk.

Very different was the behaviour of the Celtic monks whose original base lay between Ireland and Scotland. It was the Irish monastery on the island of Iona, founded by Columba, who died within a few days of Augustine's landing far to the south. A Northumbrian prince, Oswald, was a refugee on Iona during one of the many civil wars and became a Christian. When he returned to his own country as king he persuaded a saintly monk he had met on Iona, Aidan, to lead a fresh mission. Consecrated a bishop in 635, Aidan impressed because uncannily he had no interest in material rewards: when the King gave him a fine horse he gave it to a beggar, explaining that the horse was the son of a mare and the beggar a son of God. He founded a monastery at Lindisfarne. It was within reach of a protective royal castle but on a 'holy island' which recalled Iona. The Celtic monks' reputation for self-denial and prayerfulness increased through the fame of Bishop Cuthbert, an Englishman who had been a shepherd's boy. He used to pray through the night standing by the cold sea, and it was said that seals warmed his feet on the beach in the morning. Another of the treasures of the British Museum is a book: a copy of the gospels written out and 'illuminated' (decorated) by a later bishop at Lindisfarne, no doubt with assistance, early in the eighth century. The handwriting is in a beautiful Latin script also used in Ireland; the colours are varied and soft; the illustrations depict dogs and birds as well as men; the endless lines and the massed dots represent eternity. This art, an extraordinary tribute to the sanctity of the story of Christ, was created in a hut, hearing the North Sea beat on the island.

It was the good fortune of the north of England to see something of these Celtic saints when they were not praying on that beach or working in that hut, but it was also fortunate that a later Northumbrian king, Oswy, presided over a 'synod' (meeting) in Whitby on the coast of Yorkshire in 664. There it was decided to celebrate Easter on the date decreed in Rome. The Celtic missionaries had been loyal to an older calendar, but not even their holiness could prevail against the arguments in favour of accepting the Roman customs, which Oswy's queen had already insisted on keeping. As a result some of the Celtic clergy retreated to Ireland, but one of their bishops, Chad, agreed to lead the mission to the kingdom of Mercia in the Midlands. This mission was at last possible because the son and heir of the great pagan King Penda had married Oswy's daughter and become a Christian. But it was said Chad had to be pushed on to a horse for the journey: in order that they might talk with people, Celtic missionaries normally walked.

Not even on horseback could respectable women travel as missionaries, but many Christian women among the Anglo-Saxons spread their faith through their persuasive virtues as wives and mothers, and some spread it by rejecting marriage. In 679–680 two women saints died. Both had been of royal birth. Both had ruled monasteries including men: Etheldreda amid the fens at Ely, and Hilda on the cliff over the North Sea at Whitby. Both were to be remembered, for they had been almost equal in spiritual authority with an Archbishop of Canterbury who was the second founder of the English Church.

Theodore came from St Paul's birthplace, Tarsus, in what is now Turkey. He was in his late sixties when he arrived in Canterbury in 669, having been appointed by the pope since the previous archbishop had died in Rome. He worked for another 21 years with all the energy of an old man in a hurry. He toured England as an inspector, dismissing some bishops and appointing men of whom he approved. He insisted that 'dioceses' (a word which came from a division of the Roman empire) were defined areas whose bishops ought not to wander as the Celtic bishops did. He summoned the first council of the English Church, and made Canterbury such a centre of education for the clergy that students went there from Ireland; he was himself a teacher. He laid down the 'penances' to be done by sinners after a very large variety of sins; the 'penitential' which bears his name never blushes as it goes into the details. He met intense resistance but had an imperial style in these reforms and instructions. At Brixworth near Northampton a church survives from the 680s; built with Roman bricks, it resembles a *basilica*, a Roman hall for the administration of justice. Organization was being added to the charm of the Celtic saints, and when Bede wrote his book forty years later he could attempt a history of the conversion of the English people as a whole, long before England was united as one kingdom.

The best-known story in this history, completed in 731, supplies the key to an understanding of the eventual success of this difficult mission to the pagan English.

It is a story about a debate in front of Edwin, the Northumbrian king already mentioned. Those assembled listened to the preaching of Paulinus. It must have impressed them that a man coming all the way from Italy was motivated by his determination to spread his message about Christ. Bede tells of the reaction of the chief of the pagan priests, Coifi, who now revealed his dissatisfaction with the old religion: his prayers to the gods had not been answered, and he rushed out to burn the temple where he had prayed in vain. Here was the reaction of a priest meeting a superior source of supernatural power and material benefits. But 'another of the king's chief men' spoke more thoughtfully about the mystery of the meaning of human life.

For the pagan Anglo-Saxons the splendour of life lay in courage, specially courage in loyalty to one's chief in a fierce battle. They were also a people who believed in hard work with daily loyalty to the local lord; their labour on the land, clearing forests and draining marshes, began to create the English landscape. What survives of their songs and their literature – for example the great poem *Beowulf* – is usually sad: after his heroic battle with demons Beowulf perishes like everyone else. So all the courage and the work end in the dark night of death. With the bodies of their dead, or with their ashes, they buried goods which might be needed in the after-life, but the materialism of that traditional way of coping with death must have suggested to some of them that the practice was stupid. And according to Bede, what interested this landowner and warrior, at the court of King Edwin early in the seventh century, was that Paulinus spoke as a Christian missionary about life after death. Human life, this layman said, is like the swift flight of a sparrow through the hall, from door to door, leaving the dark winter on the outside and returning to it. 'Human life appears for a short space,' he reflected, 'but of what went before, or what is to follow, we know nothing'. Whether or not he reported these words accurately, Bede evidently felt that they expressed the question which the Anglo-Saxons most wanted to be answered.

He preserved the words of a song attributed to Caedmon, a servant of Whitby Abbey whose name was Celtic but who by some means acquired the techniques of Anglo-Saxon poetry. It is a song about a super-hero, the Creator. It celebrates 'the might of the Maker, the thought of his heart, the deeds of the Father of glory'. And later Anglo-Saxon poetry affirms that such a Father would not leave his children to go out into darkness like the sparrow. They tell the story of the Saviour in terms which would be understood in this society: *The Ascension of Christ* pictures his journey to heaven as being like a sea voyage, *The Fates of the Apostles* sees those brave men as the Lord's companions who were glad to fight his battles and to sacrifice their lives in his cause. But *The Dream of the Rood,* a poem written well before 750, went to what was for the Anglo-Saxons the heart of the matter. *Rod* was the Anglo-Saxon word for a cross. Here Christ is 'the young hero' who is also 'God Almighty', a warrior in the greatest of all battles, tortured on the cross, killed but not defeated, raised to immortal glory, and the poet prays that he and his friends may be carried by the cross to 'live with the High Father' in heaven 'where the Lord's army is seated at the feast'.

Anglo-Saxon Christians were willing to take the Gospel which had given a new meaning to the name of Eostre, and the Church which had brought a new hope to human life, to the lands from which their pagan ancestors had sailed to invade England.

They often did so at the risk or cost of their own lives. They were fairly safe in the area ruled by the Franks, who had now become Catholic Christians, but elsewhere no baptized king was available as their protector. Willibrord led a mission based on Utrecht, and was over eighty when he died peacefully in 739. Boniface, a man of Devon, achieved far more in his mission to what was to become Germany, organizing a Frankish Church in obedience to the popes and organizing it so effectively that he felt qualified to send to Canterbury a letter full of complaints about the English Church's laxity. In his seventies he became again a pioneering missionary, in the area where Willibrord's work had collapsed, and was murdered. Less dangerous but even more creative was the work of Alcuin, a scholar of York, who from 782 advised and assisted the great Frankish emperor Charlemagne in his policy of building up the Catholic Church in monasteries and parishes, and improving the education of the élite. The letters used in printing this book are derived from the handwriting recommended by Alcuin, who also spread the system of numbering years before or after what was believed to be the year of the birth of Christ. This *Anno Domini* system had been invented in the sixth century; Bede had used it, which was why Alcuin did.

For the rest of Anglo-Saxon history we have no narrative which may be compared with Bede's stories, and we must hurry over it.

Its worst sorrows began when in 793 the famous monastery of Lindisfarne was looted and wrecked by the pirates called Vikings. The shock of this disaster came at a time when the English Church was recovering from the disturbances caused by the attempts of Offa, king of Mercia, to conquer the whole of the country and to have his own archbishop, in Lichfield, under his thumb. Although the archbishopric of York had (at last) been established in 735, in practice the new invaders caused such devastation in the north of England that towards the end of the Anglo-Saxon period this post of leadership could be financed only by combining it with the bishopric of Worcester in the richer south. The Vikings seemed set to destroy England, as they destroyed Lindisfarne and Iona.

Having crossed the sea from Denmark and Norway, they terrorized, plundered and eventually occupied much of a country which had become virtually defenceless. During their ravages the library in York which had educated Alcuin himself was reduced to ashes, and much else of the Church whose foundation Bede had celebrated perished. These invaders met with no effective resistance until the greatest of all Anglo-Saxon kings, Alfred, ordered the towns to be fortified and organized a new army. That rally pushed the Danes back into England's eastern half, which became known as Danelaw.

An essential part of the recovery of the English was the recovery of the Church: as the word *Englisc* came into regular use, it was more or less identified with being a Christian. By the standards of his day Alfred was a scholar. That was highly unusual in a king but to him it was part of his duty to learn Latin, the Church's language, and he supervised the translation of Latin books, including Bede's history of the glorious past and the book of advice for bishops which had been written by Pope Gregory the Great: history was being mobilized like the army. In Oxford a jewel survives surrounded by gold inscribed with Alfred's name: it seems to have been a gift which was part of the propaganda for a Christian monarchy. Eventually the Danish general, acknowledging defeat, was baptized, with Alfred as his godfather. Many Danes now settled down as farmers, craftsmen or traders – and as Christians. Their conversion to the religion of the 'cross' (a Danish word like 'law') was astonishingly quick and quiet. No name of a missionary has been preserved: most of the influence must have come from the English whose lives as neighbours spoke persuasively about the power of the cross, so different from the power of the Vikings' swords and torches. Later, some English men and women went as missionaries to Denmark, to Norway and to Sweden.

Alfred's successes continued his tradition of combining military success with Christian enthusiasm. Battle by battle, all England was united under this royal house of Wessex based on Winchester: even the Viking kingdom based on York was conquered. The royal government of England became the most efficient in western Europe, and economic progress was helped by an impressive coinage of silver pounds and pennies. Laws did all that laws could do to support a morality based on the Bible, and at Bath in 973 King Edgar solemnly swore to observe and enforce these laws as part of the first elaborate coronation of an English monarch.

New dioceses were created so that bishops might lead the building of the churches and their devout use. In this period much of church life was still concentrated on the larger churches, the 'minsters', but local landlords were now taking a pride in providing a small chapel and appointing a priest to serve in it, supported by 'tithes' (a tenth of the produce) and the 'glebe' (the priest's own field). What was to become the system of dividing England into parishes was slowly beginning. The spiritual life of the Church now had a focus in monasteries where men or women (separately) prayed and worked in an expanded version of the rule drawn up for Italian monks by St Benedict. The leader in this Benedictine movement was Dunstan, the abbot of the monastery in Glastonbury who trained some of the leaders of that reform and became Archbishop of Canterbury and the king's chief adviser. But two years after his coronation by Dunstan King Edgar died. His son Edward was murdered and the great days of Anglo-Saxon England were over.

The initiative passed to a new generation of Danes, who were now able to land trained and fearsome cavalry from their long ships, and King Ethelred paid them a nation's ransom called 'Danegeld'. The intention was to bribe them to relax; the effect was to increase their appetite. Wulfstan, Archbishop of York, spoke and wrote in protest. The ideal for him was a king who would be 'Christ's substitute' and would reign in might and justice – and plainly Ethelred did not fill that role. Could anyone?

In 1016 all England acknowledged the lordship of a Danish king, Canute. This surrender seemed to be the reversal of the English Christian rally but Canute was determined to be another Alfred. He was advised by a happier Wulfstan and was himself delighted by the reception he got in Rome. He was generous to the English – too generous, allowing an Englishman to set up what became almost another kingdom as Earl of Wessex – and particularly favourable towards the English Church. Edmund, king of the East Angles, had been murdered by Danish invaders in 872; now Canute made the monastery built around his tomb (in what became Bury St Edmunds) the richest landowner in Suffolk. More recently an Archbishop of Canterbury (Alphege) had been killed by drunk Danes during a feast; now Canute allowed him to be treated like Edmund, as a saint and martyr. But this king whose reign promised so much left inferior sons. Although Ethelred's son Edward was elected king in 1042 he, too, lacked Canute's dominating ability. For example, he permitted Earl Godwin to secure the archbishopric of Canterbury for the unworthy Stigand, who was allowed to retain the wealth of the bishopric of Winchester. Edward was remembered as 'the Confessor' because he 'confessed' (expressed) his strong Christian faith, but his main achievement was to found Westminster Abbey as the church of the Christian monarchy, built in a style copied from Normandy, his mother's homeland, where he himself had been educated. He had no son and it is clear that he wished William, Duke of Normandy, to follow him on the throne of England. The Normans had been 'Northmen', in other words Viking pirates, but like the Danes in England they had been baptized and recognized as owners of land. There had been frequent civil wars between their own barons but they could combine in order to cross the Channel, and their duke had many reasons to hope that they would. They enjoyed the pope's support, partly because the character of Archbishop Stigand suggested that the Anglo-Saxon Church needed a drastic reform.

On Edward's death Harold, Earl of Wessex in succession to Godwin, acted rapidly to get himself elected king and to defeat a rebellion led by his brother, who was Earl of Northumbria. Then he marched his army some 250 miles to the south, to face an invasion commanded by Duke William. The English troops were tired and few reinforcements appeared. In a battle near Hastings, on 14 October 1066, they seemed to be prevailing until the Norman cavalry, fresh, trained and disciplined, executed a difficult manoeuvre. They pretended to retreat and, as the English pursued them, turned and massacred these men who had scented victory. Even more decisively, an arrow killed Harold, the cream of the Anglo-Saxon aristocracy died with him, and no national leader was left. An expeditionary force of about six thousand with Viking origins had done what the Danes had failed to do in Alfred's time, conquering England in the last invasion which the island was to suffer.

Pockets of resistance held out until 1072 – in London itself, in the Fens, in the north – but the Conqueror imposed order ruthlessly, and the regime included the building of large new churches, a thanksgiving to the God of battles and an announcement of the Norman's determination to remain masters.

The churches of the Anglo-Saxons, however small, had been numerous: there were more than four hundred of them in Kent alone. The stones of more than three hundred remain in English churches after nine hundred years, and one wooden church still stands (at Greensted in Essex). But after the conquest many treasures were taken from them to the churches of Normandy, where the tapestry celebrating that triumph is almost certainly the reluctant work of conscripted English women, made on the orders of Odo, Bishop of Bayeux, the Conqueror's half-brother. Other examples of the famous needlework of the Anglo-Saxons were preserved in the coffin of St Cuthbert of Lindisfarne. That became the chief treasure of Durham Cathedral, which the Normans rebuilt magnificently, next to their castle and looking rather like one. Near Cuthbert's last resting place is another shrine, containing bones believed to be those of Bede. The conquerors could demolish all the Anglo-Saxon cathedrals and destroy much of the Anglo-Saxon culture but they could not suppress the memories of the saints. Nor could they so dominate the people that the old language disappeared. It says much about daily life in the countryside after the Norman conquest that the English continued to tend animals which they continued to call cows, pigs and sheep while their French-speaking masters ate beef, pork and mutton. In the great monastery at Peterborough the chronicler of current events used Old English until 1154.

The lives of the people had been hard. Most of their cottages were made of wood with the earth as the floor, and many of the bones in their graves have been found to be full of arthritis. Most of them were dead by the age of forty, and they had probably never numbered more than a million and a half. But they had built the best run, and perhaps the richest, country in Europe at a time when Italy (for example) was in violent disorder. They could seem isolated to Catholics on the mainland but some of their leading men went on pilgrimage to Rome, their missionaries to Germany, the Netherlands and the Scandinavian countries did much to extend the authority of the popes, and it may be said that their country was as Christian as any country has ever been. The Christian religion had been accepted to an extent which was to be seen in the presence of churches in the towns and most villages and in the absence of any clear division between Church and State. Churches were the only places of drama and instruction and usually the only stone buildings; bishops were among the chief counsellors and ministers of the king; the king's council made laws about church life; the ordinary courts punished offences which were religious or moral. This mixing of Church and State was to be regarded by others as an example of the Anglo-Saxons' backwardness, but even when the Normans had set up a more distinct and elaborate structure for the Church the general idea was that a Christian king presided over a Christian country obeying the Church's laws. The idea that Jesus Christ was the supreme lord of the English also survived.

This idea had some of its roots in the Anglo-Saxon attitude that loyalty to a lord was essential and glorious, and might be rewarded by feasts and gifts. Loyalty to the Lord Christ was strong when people gained the kind of benefits which were expected by Coifi the priest from the new religion early in the seventh century. But this loyalty did not completely depend on the cause of Christ being obviously successful, as *The Dream of the Rood* showed movingly. Loyalty to Christ could endure in dark days when the Danes and Normans treated the Anglo-Saxons as brutally as the Anglo-Saxons had treated the Britons in the years of their own invasions. In adversity the English who were now Christians could feel about their duty to be loyal to the 'Lord of Heaven' what Byrthwold feels in a poem when his earthly lord has been killed in battle against the Vikings in 991:

Mind must be stronger, heart must be bolder,
Courage must be greater, as our power grows less.

3

Pastures

The Middle Ages, 1066–1530

The history of the Middle Ages had at its centre the triumph of the Catholic Church, which in England meant the victory of the faith of the Anglo-Saxons, held with great conviction in the Church which the Normans reorganized. Had the faith not been so strong, the Church would not have been so powerful; and had the Church not been so powerful, kings would have come much nearer to being dictators. As an institution the monarchy was never weak: in 1080 William the Conqueror denied that he owed allegiance to the pope, since 'I never promised it nor did any of my predecessors'. But he had been glad enough that his expeditionary force had carried a banner blessed in Rome. In 1070 a representative of the pope issued instructions that Normans who had killed Englishmen were to spend a minimum of a year as penitents, with acts as sorrowful abasement, for each life taken. How many of the Normans took any notice is not recorded, but the message had come from a gospel of justice and peace and from a Church which could not entirely forget that message. Nor could the Normans entirely forget that, with an authority derived from this message and from more worldly sources, the Church should not be ignored by the shrewd.

The Conqueror claimed that precisely because he had conquered Anglo-Saxon England the entire country belonged by right to him. Almost the whole of the old aristocracy was deprived of its wealth, and only one Englishman was allowed to function as a bishop (Wulf-stan, Bishop of Worcester). The Normans who replaced them were left in no doubt of their obligations to the king, for William had no intention of allowing the civil wars of Normandy to continue in his new kingdom. The new barons had to do homage to him, very solemnly swearing to be loyal, and when summoned to do so had to provide mounted knights who would be the most formidable part of the army at his disposal. In their turn these tenants-in-chief extracted oaths of loyalty and material support from the lesser landowners. Such was the 'feudal' system.

But William used bishops as his chief ministers. They were capable administrators; whether they were aristocrats or his own servants, they owed their promotion to him; they could be exiled if they displeased him; and although they were landowners since there was no other way of financing them, they had no legitimate sons who could inherit their estates. For the support of prayers the king relied chiefly on the monks, regarded as the cavalry of God who by their holiness would conquer sin and reach the gates of heaven with influential petitions on behalf of the rich sinners who had endowed their monasteries. The result was seen in the Domesday Book, a register of almost all the land, compiled in the 1080s. Almost a quarter of the profitable land belonged to the king and his family; almost half to the Norman lords; almost a quarter to the bishops, monks and other clergy. That was the division of the earth beneath the chant sung by the clerks before the king when he was solemnly crowned and enthroned: 'To the most serene William, the great and peace-giving king, crowned by God, life and victory!'

William chose a Norman monk, Lanfranc, as his archbishop at Canterbury, and relied on him to maintain order during his own frequent absences in Normandy. Lanfranc failed in his ambition to establish Canterbury's supremacy over the Church in Scotland and Ireland, as he also failed to end the old-fashioned practice by which many parish priests married, but he did reorganize much of Church life. Each diocese now had its centre in a town with a large cathedral where the bishop had his *cathedra* or throne; archdeacons and other officials acted as the bishops' agents; the bishops had their own courts of justice; the parishes began to have more stone churches, housing a population which slowly began to grow. The architecture of the Anglo-Norman churches was Romanesque: the massive walls and round arches recalled the severely functional buildings of the Roman empire but gradually some ornamentation was added. This addition of unnecessary art was perhaps a hint that after the semi-slavery in the years immediately following 1066 England was beginning to be somewhat merry, in the sense that its conquered people found in their religion a spring of joy as well as a source of enduring courage. It was, however, less easy for the Welsh to be at all merry. The Normans began the conquest of that proud but poor people which was completed in the fourteenth century, and the Church became part of the colonial regime. Bishops in the firmly Catholic (not Celtic) style now owed allegiance to the king and to the Archbishop of Canterbury, and the senior clergy were often absentees who despised both the land and the language of Wales. And in the twelfth century colonizing expeditions were to sail to Ireland, with results which were to be even worse for the native population. Nicholas Breakspear, the only Englishman to become pope (for five years in the 1150s), made the King of England 'overlord' of Ireland.

The Conqueror's rule might have developed into a long-lasting tyranny but some facts stood in the way. One was the fact that the kings were no more than human. England did not have a ruler with anything like the Conqueror's ability until Henry II was crowned in 1154, and after that king's death no successor had personal magnetism until the reign of a successful general, Edward I, from 1272.* The men whose lack of respect for a weak king was decisive were the barons who wanted a general to lead them, but the men who kept the government going because they could read, write, add up and think shrewdly were bishops or 'clerks' who dreamed of being bishops. These men were loyal to the Crown and looked to it for rewards, but they were also loyal to the Church which had ordained them and which was likely to be their sphere of work when they had been rewarded.

* From this point in the story Roman numerals will be used after monarchs' names: I First, II Second, III Third, IV Fourth, V Fifth, VI Sixth, VII Seventh, VIII Eighth, IX Ninth, X Tenth, XIV Fourteenth.

Monarchs who did not meet the aristocracy's requirements were not given obedience despite all the loyal promises of those who 'did homage'. The Conqueror's son, William Rufus, was almost certainly killed while hunting, on the orders of his brother and to general applause; his grand-daughter Matilda, who admittedly lacked charm, had to endure a civil war during her reign because her rival, Stephen of Blois, could make the point that she was a woman; Henry II's son Richard did nothing to improve the position of the monarchy in England by being absent on a 'crusade' in the east during most of his reign; Henry's other son John was deeply humiliated when the barons compelled him to accept Magna Carta as a guarantee of their own rights; those rights were asserted vigorously by barons in the reign of John's son, Henry III; and Edward I's son, Edward II, who like William Rufus was despised as a homosexual, was also murdered. And while monarchs rose and fell, the Church under the leadership of its bishops kept on rising.

Anselm, the Archbishop of Canterbury who had the misfortune to live in the time of William Rufus, was the greatest theologian to be produced by Western Europe in the early Middle Ages. His experience of life at the court of that king made him obstinate in defending his own position as archbishop but strangely enough it also helped his theological thinking. He restated the Church's doctrine about the basic reason for Christ's death. Anselm saw that under the feudal system tenants who failed to perform their obligations to the king and his army were required to 'give satisfaction'; and he already knew that sinners were required by the Church to 'do penance'. He therefore taught that God the Father's justice required satisfaction for the sins of the world – a penalty paid by God the Son's self-sacrifice. One reason for the welcome given to this restatement of the At-one-ment achieved by Christ was that it was believed that when the priest recited the words used during the Last Supper the bread and the wine became Christ's body and blood in their 'substance' or deepest reality although the visible 'accidents' were unchanged. The new 'substance' could be regarded as in some sense physical. The Mass could be offered to God the Father as in some sense a repetition, or at least a renewal, of the sacrifice of himself which Christ had once offered on the cross.

Lanfranc had clarified this belief about the Mass in his own theological work before becoming an archbishop. Thus between them Lanfranc and Anselm laid down foundations for the medieval Church's faith – and, incidentally, strengthened the case for forbidding priests to marry. Priests had become too special to be allowed to live like other men.

Thomas Becket, Archbishop of Canterbury in the time of Henry II, was no theologian and no saint. Before this appointment he had been a close friend of the king and an efficient minister in his government. He was appointed at Henry's wish so that he might continue to collaborate in running what had now become almost an empire, for Henry had acquired by marriage a large part of France in addition to Normandy. But Becket threw himself into every role which he played. Once he had been made England's leading bishop, his defence of the clergy's rights, in particular of his own, went beyond anything attempted by Anselm. It led to many clashes with an exasperated king, and eventually to the murder of the archbishop in his own cathedral on a December evening in 1170. The four knights who did the deed could quote an outburst of impatience which they had heard from Henry's own lips. After that death the controversial archbishop became St Thomas the Martyr. Among the first of the pilgrims who flocked to his tomb was his outwardly penitent king. So his tomb became a rich shrine and a magnet almost equal in prestige with the greatest centres to which medieval Christians went on pilgrimage: Jerusalem, Rome and Compostela in Spain.

The disputes in his confrontation with Henry were not vitally important: mainly they resulted from the king's wish that his own judges should punish 'clerks' convicted of crimes in the bishop's courts. (These clerks did not have to prove their innocence when accused: it was enough if they could assemble neighbours who could testify that their guilt was unlikely. Even if proved guilty, their worst fate would be the bishop's prison. And they did not have to be priests: all that was essential was that they should be either 'tonsured' with a special haircut or at least able to read a few words of a psalm in Latin.) After Becket's martyrdom Henry had to abandon his plan but during many years to come royal officials found quiet ways of making life very difficult for clerical criminals. That was also true about criminals who were not clerks but who could escape hanging by taking refuge in a 'sanctuary' provided by a church: after a pause they usually had to accept life imprisonment in the sanctuary's own prison, or leave the country, or face starvation. The underlying question in this dispute between archbishop and king, however, was whether the Church was able to set limits to the power of the monarchy. No one who witnessed the pilgrimages to Canterbury could doubt that many of the English hoped that it would be able. The details of the conflicts between archbishops and kings probably did not interest them: what attracted was the simple thought that an archbishop had been willing to sacrifice his life in the defence of a Church which included them. And although Becket's parents were Normans, his popularity as a martyred saint was a sign that the Church which the Normans had reshaped now belonged to the English people.

Stephen Langton was Archbishop of Canterbury in the time of King John, against the king's wishes. He was a scholar (the first to divide the Bible into verses easy to quote) who was appointed by Pope Innocent III in defiance of John's plan to arrange the appointment of his own secretary. The consequent dispute resulted in an 'interdict' by which the pope prohibited almost all services in England's churches over four years, but eventually John surrendered and did homage to Innocent III. When Langton took up his responsibilities as archbishop, he saw it as his duty to be a leader of the barons who extracted from the King the concessions recorded in the great charter, *Magna Carta* (1215). But he was no democrat: he defended the royal rights of Henry III when the barons attempted to push their way beyond the settlement of 1215. And the leader of those rebellious aristocrats, Simon de Montfort, was no democrat either: his only connection with democracy was the development of a 'parliament' (consultation) occasionally enlarging the king's council by summoning extra support from the higher clergy and others among the rich during these troubled years.

The chief task of a parliament was to vote the taxes needed by the king's government and army. A more prosperous England used money more frequently, and coins were even more useful than the knights provided by the feudal system, in the making of an army whose chief strength now lay in the skill of its paid archers. However, from about

1350 the clergy successfully maintained that they had the right to decide their own 'subsidies' to the government, rather than paying taxes like the laity.

A more prosperous England could also afford to pay for the making of very beautiful churches to match the great Gothic churches being built in France. Soon after the famous martyrdom a fire destroyed much of Canterbury Cathedral, which could be rebuilt gloriously thanks to the income from the flourishing cult of St Thomas. The arches which added interest to the walls were now becoming pointed, and the glass which filled the larger windows was now coloured and painted (in Canterbury with scenes of miracles rewarding sick pilgrims). The climax of this 'Early English' style in architecture was to come in the new cathedral built in Salisbury 1220–58. In the same period the west front of the lovely cathedral in Wells was enriched by a series of more than 350 life-sized statues, including statues of the Anglo-Saxon saints. But the English did not rest content with that beauty. In 1250 Henry III began the reconstruction of Westminster Abbey, with the shrine of Edward the Confessor behind the high altar, and made it his chief interest while king. Twenty years later the reconstruction of Exeter Cathedral began as another climax of the 'Decorated' style. In the first half of the next century many churches already standing were wholly or partly rebuilt in this style, often with the addition of a Lady Chapel in honour of the mother of Jesus, and new churches were added. By now London had some forty thousand inhabitants and more than a hundred churches. Norwich and York each had almost ten thousand people and more than twenty-five churches.

The wealth which paid for all that work by masons and other highly skilled craftsmen came from the labours of a larger population which farmed strips in large fields in addition to the smallholdings around the cottages of the 'manor'. It also came from the wool trade, for hundreds of thousands of sheep grazed on the pastures provided by land which could not be ploughed easily. One reason for gifts to the Church was that people wanted the clergy to pray for their own souls after death and for the souls of those they loved. Another reason was the ability of the Church to frighten the living: ashes put on parishioners each Ash Wednesday were reminders that their bodies would soon return to dust, and in many churches there was a wall-painting of the Last Judgement, the Day of Doom, showing the fate of sinners condemned to the everlasting tortures of hell. But the things of beauty in the churches were not created by people who were merely terrified.

In Rome in 1215 the Fourth Lateran Council, launching an international programme of reforms, decreed that all marriages should take place before a priest, and that at least once a year (usually at Easter) every parishioner should confess his or her sins to a priest before receiving communion from him. In the parish church every child was baptized; in its churchyard everyone was buried; processions went from it to ask for God's blessing on the crops. The drinking of ale around a bonfire celebrated festivals. The clergy were there and (it was thought) would always be there, but the homeliness of medieval religion was illustrated by the system of encouraging a boy to act as a bishop on St Nicholas's day. The clergy did not get too angry when on occasion people made fun: the fun was within a family, within an unquestioned faith. In Lent everyone went without luxuries but it was the time of year when food was scarcer anyway although the days were lengthening; on Palm Sunday everyone 'crept' to the cross and kissed it; at Easter there were games with eggs and flowers; in the autumn everyone remembered the dead. So in the countryside or in the expanding towns, every little community took a pride in the church building, in its contents and in its customs. As one looks back from a very different England, one is likely to be struck by the abundance of good design and craftsmanship (in a population less than a tenth of the size it was to reach in the twentieth century), as well as by the abundance of the piety. In Southwell Minster (now the Anglican cathedral for Nottinghamshire) the Chapter House seems to embody the unity in the spirit of the high Middle Ages. As the clergy met in that room, around them were carved leaves which preserve for ever the countryside of the 1290s: leaves of oak, ivy, rose, vine, buttercup and hop. As Sir Nikolaus Pevsner wrote in the 1940s, the sculptors seem to have been inspired by 'the conviction that so much beauty can exist only because God is in every man and beast, in every herb and stone'.

In many other ways England took a leading part in the creative liveliness of Catholicism in the high Middle Ages. When the

Benedictine monasteries grew so rich that many of their monks became absorbed in the supervision of work done by others on their estates, the Cistercian monks built new abbeys outside the towns and the cultivated areas. Lay 'brothers' toiled manfully in the fields, and the priests responsible for the worship lived very simply. When the parish priests could not cope with the population in the towns, from the 1220s the Franciscan and Dominican friars began to care and to preach, in their early years sharing the poverty of the most humble. The Franciscans had been founded by the much loved St Francis of Assisi in Italy; the more scholarly Dominicans by a Spaniard who saw the urgent need for preachers. When the Church needed a better educated clergy, the universities of Oxford and Cambridge began to turn boys, often poor boys, into graduates. And gradually these move-ments and institutions began to experience the problems and tempta-tions of wealth, because they were so successful. The Cistercians did much for agriculture and became almost as rich as the older monas-teries: the ruins of the great churches which they built at Fountains and Rievaulx are still among the sights of Yorkshire. The friars won the grateful love of so many in the laity that, receiving many gifts, they were taken away from their original mission. They went to the universities in order to recruit but they became teachers themselves – and bishops. Roger Bacon, the first English scientist, was a Franciscan friar, speculating and experimenting in Oxford.

The boom in Church and State did not last. The population was already beginning to outrun the food supply when the weather wors-ened and agriculture suffered; and in 1348 a succession of plagues originating in Asia, the 'Black Death', began their devastation. These epidemics reduced the population by about a third, and numbers did not climb again for another hundred years. The Church suffered along with the people. Taxation had been increased in order to pay for wars of conquest in Scotland under Edward I and in France under Edward III – and since large armies of occupation could not be afford-ed, now the conquests could not be kept. A smaller labour force objected to a 'poll' tax being demanded from everyone and to legisla-tion which tried to prevent wages rising. In 1381 a peasants' revolt was encouraged by some of the clergy, men who were themselves poor, but was suppressed by the landowners, including bishops. In London the mob which had killed an archbishop was stopped from further rioting by the cool courage of the boy king, Richard II. Within twenty years Richard was to be starved to death after imprisonment by a rebel who became the first of the Lancastrian kings, Henry IV. He was not then saved by his courage – or by his taste for the beautiful and the civilized. The lovely Wilton Diptych which was painted for an altar in his chapel is a treasure of the National Gallery in London, and he was the first Englishman known to have used a handkerchief.

Little happiness was spread by the teaching of John Wyclif, an Oxford theologian. At first he was taken up by lay aristocrats, for he condemned the wealth of the Church: wealth which the aristocracy wished to spend for their own purposes, including the war in France. Then he was dropped by these patrons, partly because he was associated (however unfairly) with the peasants' revolt but mainly because his own revolt against the official Church became extreme: he advocated a simpler, more biblical, more moral, religion without what seemed to him the magic in the Mass and the corruption of the whole system of religion controlled by the pope and the priests. In the end he had to leave Oxford, and after his death in 1384 his followers, the Lollards, became an underground movement among the poor, using a Bible translated into English. A few were burned as heretics. Although the sufferings of these victims and the public penitence of those who did not persist in heresies seem to have aroused little public sympathy, the bishops were sufficiently alarmed to forbid the making of any official English Bible: 'simple' folk might get strange ideas unless guided about Scripture's meaning.

The discontent which continued in England during the fifteenth century was economic, not religious, since the peasants' grievances had not been met, and many landlords now began to increase these grievances by 'enclosing' (treating as their own property) fields which in the old days had been open to all. The civil wars between Lancastrians and Yorkists, struggling for the throne, did not help. Yet if the country was not the 'merry England' of later legend, neither was it miserable. This was the period when *caroles* were sung (often as music for dancing) to celebrate Christmas or Easter or the coming of spring, and the many Latin phrases in them showed that the Church's services were part of what inspired a joy which survived wars and plagues, grievances and rebellions.

A small collection of masterpieces about the life of private prayer survives from the fourteenth century. Richard Rolle, a hermit who lived alone, advertised the delights of loving God in *The Fire of Love*. Walter Hinton wrote more soberly about the patience in action and contemplation needed to climb *The Ladder of Perfection*. An anonymous priest wrote *The Cloud of Unknowing:* to follow Christ perfectly is 'a full great travail', to love God is to encounter the One who is No-thing, No-where, and it is to find that 'by love he may be gotten and holden, but by thought never'. And an anonymous woman who lived and prayed alone, known to later generations as Mother Julian of Norwich, wrote *Revelations of Divine Love*, the first book in English by a woman. She had looked very deeply into a crucifix when thought to be dying in 1373. She wrote the first version of her thoughts quite quickly, but the full version was not completed for another twenty years. She found a motherly tenderness in Jesus and used that as the key to the mystery of God: 'Love was his meaning. Who showed it thee? Love. What showed he thee? Love.'

Other books which have become famous were written in English and were full of a Christian attitude to English humanity. William Langland, for example, spent much of his life in London and in poverty, but he told of a dream of a 'field full of folk'. His vision included many who did not deserve to be called Christians but also 'Piers Ploughman' (who gave his name to this great poem). Piers leads the search for Truth and Love and is disappointed by the Church but is then met by Christ, himself dressed as a labourer. He glimpses a great barn called Unity, built for 'brethren of one blood: alike beggars and earls'. When the dreamer awakes he finds that it is Easter morning and the bells are ringing for church.

Geoffrey Chaucer had a richer lifestyle than Langland, as a successful civil servant, and an imagination so rich that John Dryden was to call it 'God's plenty'. His *Canterbury Tales* imagined a great variety of pilgrims on the road to Becket's shrine. Thrown together all were in 'fellowshippe' as they told a great variety of tales, often earthy and often funny. Chaucer was very much a layman but he ended his book with the Parson's Tale, a dull sermon by a good man. The others had fallen silent: the nun who was devoted to 'smale houndes', the monk who was a country gentleman, the friar who 'knew the tavernes wel', the seller of pardons ('indulgences') who obviously needed pardon, the much-married Wife of Bath who would not 'live parfitly', the 'clerk of Oxenford' who loved books more than money, the honest ploughman, the 'varray parfit gentil knight', the parson himself, who lived as he taught.

Not many of the English used the Church for prayer at the level of the great spiritual writers, while many did complain about the failures of the clergy to live as they preached, but a great mass of evidence indicates that almost everyone was fairly content to end up in church like Langland's dreamer and Chaucer's pilgrims.

Towards the end of the Middle Ages more people than before were able to read and write, even to think for themselves, but even in this élite dissent from the Church's teaching was not frequent. Some evidence comes from the wills which the well-to-do made as death drew near. Almost always these documents were emphatically devout and often they expressed their piety by gifts to the poor as well as to the Church. The dying must have been influenced by the fact that a priest or 'clerk' was taking down their words and was able to censor them, but the evidence has some value. Other evidence comes from the books which could be bought when the new technology of printing reached England: William Caxton began printing in 1476, in the shadow of Westminster Abbey. Many of these books were devotional, and even the main alternative, romantic tales of chivalry and courtly love, always had Christian ideas or customs in the background. And when not on their deathbeds or buried in a book, most of the English, rich or poor, able to read or illiterate, still showed quite happily a practical acceptance of the Church's authority.

Although there were some clocks, the time of day or night was usually stated by a reference to one of the Church's many daily services. All work was meant to stop on a Sunday and often did. Almost fifty weekdays in the year were 'holy days', saints' days or other festivals meant to be treated like Sundays. On Fridays and almost seventy other days adults were obliged to fast, avoiding meat, eggs and cheese. Goods were meant to be sold at a 'just' price; usually it was the price suggested by the market, but not always. Usury (the taking of interest on loans) was forbidden in theory and excessive interest could bring trouble to a capitalist. It was accepted that the Church's courts had jurisdiction in all cases concerning marriages, morality and sworn promises. Above all, it was accepted that Christ and his saints were very real, very near and very active.

Christianity was then what science was to be in the twentieth century: always there in the background. People did not have to live up to all its teachings but they were impressed on the occasions when its power was revealed and almost the whole community joined in expressions of agreement and admiration. In some of the leading towns enthusiastic amateurs performed plays based on the Bible or on the Church's moral teaching, and crowds enjoyed them as they were taken through the streets on carts. Crowds also assembled eagerly to hear special preachers. Although most parish priests made no attempt at eloquence, they might read out their versions of the collection of specimen sermons made by John Mirk. For the laity there were two great moments in the Mass (although they were often urged to be attentive and prayerful in their own ways throughout the service). One was the crisis when the 'host', the bread which was the Body, was elevated: people talked about 'seeing God' and were expected to pray fervently. This bread was too holy to be eaten by the congregation more than once a year, and the laity were not allowed to drink the wine, but earlier in the service came another solemn moment. The *pax* (a piece of wood painted with a Christian symbol) was passed round for everyone to kiss: it was a moment of a parish's unity and much emphasis was placed on being reconciled with neighbours. After the Mass 'holy bread' was distributed: the loaf was less holy than the 'host' but was another symbol of unity.

In 1436 Margery Kempe, who could not read or write, began to dictate the story of her life to a priest. The autobiography was virtually unknown until an early copy of this manuscript came to light five hundred years later. It was the story of a highly emotional woman who lived in Norfolk (and visited Mother Julian, to be told that what mattered was 'charity'). In her early years she was extravagant (and failed to make money by running little businesses to meet her debts) and lustful (she and her husband had fourteen children) but eventually she renounced sex and entered a life of churchgoing, pilgrimages and ecstasies, visions and conversations with Christ and the saints. She was allowed to receive Holy Communion every Sunday, when normally the laity were expected to do no more than attend and adore, but the clergy were less pleased by her habit of tears whenever she saw a crucifix or heard a sermon about her Lord's suffering. She cried out in anger whenever she saw a child or a horse hit. She was thoroughly orthodox but a thorough nuisance in her eagerness. When the Archbishop of York told her that he heard that she was a wicked woman, she replied that she had heard that he was a wicked man. When the Archbishop of Canterbury interviewed her, she questioned him about his soul and about his employment of men who swore. And we know that she was not alone in having a religion which was dominated by Christ, not by the clergy, yet which met Christ in the Church.

In 1354 Henry, Duke of Lancaster, dictated to his chaplain a self-examination which seems to be sincere both in his feeling that he needed forgiveness and in his memory of enjoying a far from perfect life. He accuses himself of avoiding the stench of the poor and of loving wines and sauces, flowers and fruit, the kisses of women and his bed. He has taken too much pride in the strength of his arms and in the rings on his fingers. Now he needs Christ's sweat of agony on the cross as a sick man needs a broth or a hot bath, and he must hunt for his sins as a hound sniffs to find the fox. If English people in the lower ranks of society had been able to express themselves in language which has survived, presumably their tone about their own daily lives would have been much the same as the duke's: penitent but not entirely regretful. But the approach of death, leading to heaven (usually via 'purgatory' where sins would be punished in painful detail) or hell, was not taken lightly.

The deathbeds of medieval Christians had always been places of drama and solemnity as priest, family and friends joined the dying in prayers of penitence and petition, but the Black Death began a period when there was increased emphasis on prayers, including many

Masses, to ask for mercy on the dead. It was now becoming customary for people on specially good terms with the clergy to be buried within a church, but bishops were among those who ordered that a rotting corpse should be carved on their tombs. It was a reminder that all must die, yet all can pray for the dead. Many priests were appointed whose main duty was to say these prayers in chapels called 'chantries', although they also did other church work. Many laymen joined fraternities whose main purpose, in addition to socializing, was to arrange funerals and prayers for the dead. They had to arrange them with the clergy, who therefore did not feel insecure when rebuked by the likes of Margery Kempe. Seven years after his recorded self-examination, his chaplain had to take the duke's funeral: he was a victim of the Black Death. The clergy seemed as secure as the system which they operated; a system stronger than death, for their forgiveness of sins brought God's eternal forgiveness whatever punishments had still to be endured in purgatory, and suffering in purgatory could be reduced by prayers on earth.

In the fifteenth century the history of the monarchy was often bloodstained. Henry IV seems to have known, with some penitence, that he was responsible for the death of the legitimate king of England, but Henry V claimed to be also the rightful king of France, launching another invasion which (like Edward III's) came to nothing despite its cruelty and expense. Henry VI did not look like a king; his dress was shabby, his tongue was foolish. Judged unfit to reign over an England where many soldiers were home from the war in France, he was deposed and murdered. The Duke of York who overthrew him was the tall, manly, clever, charming and ruthless Edward IV, with a mother and a sister who were exceptionally devout, as he certainly was not. He had a brother executed for treason and an Archbishop of York imprisoned (who died of the shock). He was the only successful Yorkist king: another brother (almost certainly) had the young Edward V murdered, and as the notorious Richard III was defeated and killed in a rebellion supporting the claims of Henry Tudor, in 1485.

The popes, too, were often in trouble. Hopes that they might again become the leaders of religious vitality in a united Church revived when they returned to Rome after a long period when they had set up their court and bureaucracy in Avignon in the south of France but then, for some thirty years, there were rival popes, backed respectively by England and by France. When that 'great schism' was ended in 1417 by a council of the Church, a long disagreement between councils and popes lasted for another thirty years. Then the popes of the Renaissance became obsessed by the need for money to support their more-than-princely position. But just as we should resist the temptation to imagine that England was always 'merry', so we should reject any tendency to think that it was becoming republican or Protestant.

However bloodstained individual kings might be, in life or death, the institution of the monarchy was, like the institution of the papacy, surrounded by clouds of incense. When the tomb of the murdered Edward II drew pilgrims and their money to Gloucester Cathedral, it became possible to rebuild in the new Perpendicular style which was unique to England. In this style the decoration was elegant: severe rectangles on the walls surrounded large windows, and pillars soared straight to the intricate vaulting in the stone roofs. In the same style Henry VI, who genuinely loved piety and learning, built huge college chapels for his foundations in Eton and Cambridge; and Edward IV, who arranged his murder, also arranged for the building of St George's Chapel in Windsor Castle, where Richard III had Henry VI buried as part of his own bid for respectability. And actions by the senior clergy expressed the same belief as these buildings did: the Crown was at the summit of the social order which God had ordained. The bishops greatly admired the orthodox but brutal Henry V and remained loyal to his pious but incompetent son. The same Archbishop of Canterbury, an aristocrat who had been a bishop since the age of 25, crowned and anointed Edward IV, Richard III and Henry VII, transmitting the mystique of the monarchy from the Yorkists to the Tudors.

The king and the pope were then almost always allies. Parliament passed statutes (Acts) prohibiting the reception of papal decisions and 'provisions' (appointments) in England without the king's consent, but in practice this legislation produced a workable compromise. The king nominated men to England's seventeen diocesan bishoprics, for he needed administrators who could do the work of government in

Church and State alike, and the pope appointed them without a fuss. The king and the pope shared the advantages to be gained from appointing their servants to canonries in cathedrals. For these practical purposes, therefore, the pope's power was limited by the royal government; yet in matters of religion he was fully accepted as the supreme authority, and even in details of local church life decisions were often left to his officials. The English Church had no national council, since from Anglo-Saxon times it had been divided into two provinces, that of Canterbury and that of York, with only three dioceses in the poorer north; Canterbury's archbishop was the 'Primate of All England' but the two were more or less equal. In the Church's theory only the pope held the provinces together. When the bishops were not immersed in political work (which in practice brought them together as Englishmen) they were essentially judges enforcing the laws of the Catholic Church. No adequate provision was made for the training of parish priests, but the archdeacons were supposed to carry out 'visitations' of all the parishes every year, seeking out faults and sins to report to other officials of the bishop.

The more sacramental side of a diocesan bishop's work was usually delegated to an obscure assistant bishop, often a Franciscan friar or an Irishman willing to accept low pay, but this practice did not indicate any lack of respect for the Church's sacramental system or for the priesthood which operated it. As the population recovered from the long-term effects of the Black Death, the recruitment of clergy also recovered. In the 1520s there seem to have been about forty thousand priests in the parishes and about ten thousand in the monasteries. The Church was in fact overstaffed and this brought problems. Too many of the 'chantry' priests responsible for Masses on behalf of the dead had no clear duties to the living, and too many of the monasteries, which had no clear duties beyond prayer and which numbered about eight hundred, were too small to be proper communities. And the institutions which had been creative in the years before the Black Death had now become too privileged and wealthy. In most monasteries enthusiasm had declined although there was, it seems clear, less immorality than was alleged in gossip. A large share of the tithes which ought to have provided incomes for pastors resident in every parish had been 'appropriated' (diverted) to the support of the monks, so that in many parishes there was a 'vicar' (substitute) instead of a proper 'rector' who might have had more commitment. Many parishes in the north were too large for proper pastoral care, although there people could use the monasteries and chantries for regular worship, and (as events were to show) had more affection for them than was normal in southern England. In the towns the churches of the friars were often more popular than the parish churches but one result was that the friars, like the monks, had at least the reputation of being too money-minded. A university course was long and could be financed by an appointment to a parish where the graduate had no intention of residing. The course itself often led to a study of theology or of the Church's law, and both subjects had at least the reputation of being hair-splitting.

Although before the 1540s England had no equivalent to the Protestants of Germany and Switzerland, who dramatically and decisively attacked the whole system of the medieval Church, the nature of the popularity of that system made a few of the English uneasy. John Colet became the dean of St Paul's Cathedral in London and would have been horrified to be accused of heresy, but he did lecture on St Paul's letters in Oxford and caused some excitement by going straight to the New Testament without much attention to traditional medieval interpretations, and he did rebuke his fellow clergy for being too worldly. A lawyer, Thomas More, who was to be involved in the burning of heretics and was to die rather than say that the pope was not the Church's head on earth, wrote *Utopia* about an imaginary island. He wrote it in Latin but included thinly disguised criticisms of Church and State in the England around him in the 1510s: in Utopia religion was tolerant because reasonable and priests were few because all were holy. It was said that another layman, Thomas Linacre, who founded the Royal College of Physicians, read the New Testament in Greek for the first time not long before his death in 1524, and remarked: 'Either this is not the Gospel or we are not Christians.'

For this highly popular religious system could be criticized or totally condemned then or later. It could be objected that faith in Christ as the living Saviour was obscured by all the emphasis on the power of the saints, particularly Christ's mother, and by all the images showing his weakness, as a child on his mother's lap or as a victim dying on a cross. It could be said that too many stories were told of visions which proved that inside the 'host' consecrated by the priest in the Mass there was Christ's bleeding body in physical reality. Too many legends were told of miracles of healing, fertility or deliverance from demons – and it was too often said that the miracles had been achieved by uttering the name of Jesus, by a rapid prayer to a favourite saint, by ringing church bells (believed to be effective defences during thunderstorms), by sprinkling holy water or by lighting a candle. Too often it was taught and believed, in the interpretation of an 'indulgence', that the Church had the power to release penitent sinners from a stated number of days of suffering in purgatory after death; and that an acceptable way of expressing penitence, even on another's behalf, was a financial gift to the Church before death. Too often an image in a church was given so much honour (for example, by the burning of many 'lights' before it) that the transcendence of God over all images was left in the dark or forgotten. Too often it was thought that salvation could be earned by performing the 'works' which the Church encouraged. Too often the mystery of eternity was domesticated, although at the same time the clergy attacked popular magic or superstition which they did not control. (The 'exorcism' or expulsion of demons, for example, ought to be carried out by a priest using a formula approved by the Church.) If this was corruption it was the price paid for the Church's immense popularity.

Any claim that England was seething with religious discontent goes against most of the evidence. In the churches there was much building, rebuilding or extension. In the 1490s a great new central tower was added to Canterbury Cathedral. Although faced with stone it used half a million bricks, and like the new towers of many parish churches it proclaimed the assurance of the Catholic Church – an assurance which was being dramatized by the new festival of Corpus Christi, when the Body of Christ was carried in procession round the streets, so that all might adore. The same confident message was conveyed by the sumptuous Lady Chapel which Henry VII ordered to be built as an extension to Westminster Abbey. It was begun in 1503 and the king's own body was brought to it for burial in 1509. In his life-time Henry Tudor had resolved to stay on the throne which he had seized, and he had shrewdly concentrated on securing his government's financial strength. Now it seemed that he was determined to purchase the kingdom of heaven. A splendid tomb was made for his body, and the will of this king, who was reputed to be a miser, ordered that ten thousand Masses were to be paid for, at twice the normal rate, as prayers for the happy repose of his soul. Silver boxes to hold the consecrated wafer which was the Body of Christ were to be placed in all parish churches which did not possess one.

The arrangements surrounding the pious death of the first of the Tudor monarchs made it obvious that the Catholicism which the Normans had reorganized in England was very much alive. It was supported by an elaborate theology and by the alliance of Church and State to suppress heresy; by the expensive devotion of the highest in the land and of the laity in nine thousand parishes; by the participation of the whole community in fasts and feasts. If it was vulnerable to criticism, the criticism had to be directed against the very practices which had made it so very popular. Before the sudden thunderstorm which destroyed it, the medieval Catholic Church looked as secure as a lushly green pasture on a summer's day.

4

Clouded Hills

Reformations, 1530–1715

If we connect William Blake's mythological poem with the real history of England, we may perhaps say that some 'mountains' of spiritual heroism were reached by the saints of Anglo-Saxon England, and that 'pastures' were enjoyed by the Church in the Middle Ages. Now we can look at 'hills'. Less lofty than the mountains of a past which was distant, and considerably less comfortable than the recently enjoyed pastures, nevertheless a succession of crises stood above the routine of the years somewhat as hills rise above a level plain. Between 1530 and 1715 there was no single 'Reformation' but Christianity was reshaped, and reshaped again, and nothing was settled until the end of the period (only to be unsettled after it). Almost all of the English were then Christians, and some were Christians who lived and died with great courage in order to practise and defend their version of the faith, but if we are to be honest we must also say that their minds were clouded by hatreds. They were often brave under persecution but when they had their opportunity they, too, were intolerant: that, too, seemed to be their religious duty. And often they would think it their duty to use force.

Because reform and politics seemed indivisible, a Catholic loyal to the pope could find that being Roman meant agreeing that a Protestant should be replaced on the throne, if necessary by means of murder, rebellion or invasion. A Protestant determined to see the country purified could also accept a duty to rebel against the monarchy – or, in some cases, against the whole social order. But the Church of England, the official Church which tried to be both Catholic and Protestant and to include the whole nation, emerged triumphant from these conflicts because a greater force was on its side: it was controlled and therefore supported by the men who owned the land and were the government.

However, to admit all that truth is not to deny that many English Christians rose to heroism when force was used against them. As we look back from a different age we probably find it hard to understand why they did not respect people with consciences as strong as their own; why they did not distinguish more clearly between Church and State; why they could not see that faith meaning trust in Christ is essential to the fully Christian life but to be genuine must be followed by a serious effort to live that life; why they could not agree that the Bible is vitally important but not the only source of Christian belief, and that for the faithful the presence of Christ in the Eucharist is real but not physical. But at the time it appeared that two Christianities, two incompatible visions of God and good, were at war – and on both sides it was thought to be a war in which lives ought both to be given and to be taken.

During the sixteenth century about three hundred English people were burned alive as heretics on the government's orders after condemnation by Catholic bishops. They were 'Protestants', so named after the protest in Germany against attempts to suppress the 'heresies' which Martin Luther began to expound in the 1510s. John Foxe told the story of their ordeals in his *Book of Martyrs* first published in English in 1563. An earlier and smaller book in Latin had made a knowledge of the courageously obstinate Lollards available to Europe, but the main part of Foxe's immensely influential history was propaganda about the heroism of the martyrs in the reign of a Catholic queen, Mary (1553–58). In an age when even men were not expected to argue against the authorities, it was specially striking that 55 of the martyrs were women. Five were bishops, including Thomas Cranmer, who had been Henry VIII's agent as Archbishop of Canterbury, and the prominent reforming bishops Ridley and Latimer, but most were lay men, often of little education, or parish priests. Their deaths damaged the Catholic Church's popularity more than the executions of the Lollards had done: one reason was that the government stupidly allowed the victims to preach their message appealing to the Bible before the flames silenced them, after an agony often prolonged because the wood was damp. Latimer had been a mighty and popular preacher in pulpits, but most memorably he now said to his trembling companion: 'Be of good comfort, Master Ridley. We shall this day light such a candle by God's grace in England as I trust shall never be put out.'

While England was ruled by Mary's Protestant half-sister, Elizabeth I, more than a hundred Roman Catholic priests were hanged when they had been hunted down, usually after severe tortures. They, too, bore witness to a courageous faith and they inspired lay women and men, old or young, who were also to be honoured among these 189 martyrs. Many thousands of English Catholics loyal to the pope were willing to incur heavy fines and to run greater risks as 'recusants', people who refused to attend the Protestant services held in their parish churches, now stripped of their medieval beauty. Punishment could mean also the fate of being thought traitors. The religion which had seemed impregnable in the 1520s was very dangerous to its adherents half a century later. Robert Coulton, a simple boy, when examined by the Protestant Archbishop of Canterbury and other elders, replied: 'I hear say that England hath been a Catholic Christian country a thousand years afore this queen's reign and her father's. If that were the old highway to heaven, then why should I forsake it? I pray you give me leave to save my soul.'

But in practice persecution, whether Catholic or Protestant, was patchy since England had no police force, and much depended on local magistrates, who had their own likes and dislikes, and on their often lazy or corrupt constables. In the main, at ground level, the history of religion in sixteenth-century England was not a history of idealism and heroism. Being human, most people seem to have adjusted their religion to what was favoured by the government of the day, and kept their thoughts to themselves. Probably the most genuinely Christian lives were those of 'pious' women who would have been expected to be quiet and to avoid controversy even in less dangerous times. There is a moving similarity between the surviving pieces of evidence about such women, whether Catholic, Anglican or more definitely Protestant: in them all we see the practices of prayer and charity combined with the running or work of a household, itself regarded as obedience to God's laws. Wealthier women were expected to read religious books and to give religious instruction to children and servants (as men who were employers were expected to instruct any apprentices). The discipline in many such lives could explain why, when challenged, a few women were prepared to be as cour-ageous as the men amid the flames, on the executioner's scaffold or in prison.

Yet people who safely conformed were of course more typical. Vicar Aleyn of Bray in Berkshire submitted to every change in the country's official religion, from the reign of Henry VIII to that of Elizabeth I. When he was taunted about this lack of principle, he replied: 'Not so, for I have always kept my principle, which is this, to live and die the Vicar of Bray' (according to Thomas Fuller in the next century). In 1601 this was attributed to a layman, a fictitious character in a book which tried to sum up popular reactions to the theological arguments: 'Well, I cannot read, and therefore I cannot tell what Christ or what St Paul may say, but this I am sure of, that God is a good man (worshipped might he be), he is merciful, and that we must be saved by our good prayers and good serving of God.' The accounts kept by the churchwardens who were responsible for the care of the fabric of the parish churches show that they paid carpenters and masons to remove the 'images' which a Protestant government condemned as 'idols', and hid many of them while selling others. They paid for them to be replaced under a Catholic government, only to have to make a third payment for their removal under Elizabeth a few years later. And it has been suggested that one reason why many people such as the churchwardens eventually accepted the government's version of Protestantism was that although it was more boring it was also cheaper than medieval Catholicism.

No doubt the frequency of such changes produced some cynicism about religion itself, in addition to a heroism which made fanatics as well as martyrs, but the main impression left by the detailed examination of the local evidence which historians undertook in the second half of the twentieth century was that through all the revolutions most of the English, women and men, remained Christian without much theology. The religion of the people was mainly practical and moral, and it kept this character as its practices gradually shifted from not eating meat on Fridays because the Church taught the duty to fast, to not eating it because the government protected the livelihood of fishermen; from ringing bells as religion to ringing bells as a team-sport; from some prayers during sacraments to some attention during sermons; from quoting the Latin Mass in carols to quoting the English Bible in discussions about all manner of subjects. The courts of the bishops continued to try to punish people who defamed their neighbours or who were friendly to the point of fornication or adultery, and attempts were made to empty alehouses during the hours of church services. Family life and earning one's living as respectably as possible made up most of what was reckoned to be 'good serving of God'. But if we ask why popular religion gradually took a more Protestant than Catholic shape, there seem to be some true answers. Protestantism became identified with patriotism after a long period when the national government rejected the papacy and locally the power was in hands which had picked up wealth from the collapse of the medieval Church. The Bible's authority and influence did much to replace the attractiveness of the Church's rituals. The spread of education did much to persuade people that such rituals had attracted only unenlightened minds. And sensitive Christians found it a great relief to think that all their sins could be fully forgiven 'for the sake of Jesus Christ our Saviour', without the punishments in purgatory which in the doctrine of the medieval Church remained necessary after the priest's pronouncement of forgiveness. But none of these changes took place overnight.

* * *

In the 1520s and 1530s there was little attempt or desire to defend the clergy against the government of Henry VIII. The House of

Commons joined in protests against practices in the bishops' courts. One notorious case had been the prosecution of a merchant in London for refusing to hand over to his parish priest the robe in which his baby son, now dead, had been christened; the offending father had been found dead while in the Church's custody. There was also now some feeling against the bishops who were energetically demanding the burning of heretics and their books lest the infection of Martin Luther's ideas should spread to England from Germany. Few tears were shed when Cardinal Thomas Wolsey, who drew the incomes of a number of rich bishoprics but spent most of his time as the king's chief minister, fell from power. In 1531 representatives of the clergy agreed to pay a large sum to the government on the ground that they had broken English law by accepting Wolsey as the pope's representative without the king's written consent; the real reason why they were in no position to resist (although they tried to bargain) was that they were generally believed to have surplus wealth.

When Henry demanded recognition as 'Supreme Head' of the English Church in the crisis of 1531–34, almost all the clergy assented or kept silent, adding 'as far as the law of Christ allows' in order to satisfy their consciences as well as their king. They could tell themselves that it would not be a momentous change to end what there was of jurisdiction by the pope, a remote figure. Bishop Stephen Gardiner, who was to become a persecutor of Protestants, wrote a book defending the king's new title. The only prominent men who paid for their refusals with their lives were a bishop (John Fisher of Rochester, who argued theologically) and a layman, Thomas More, who had replaced Wolsey as the king's chief minister. When in 1536–40 first the smaller and then the larger monasteries were forced to surrender their buildings and estates in exchange for pensions, the rebellion in the north called the Pilgrimage of Grace could be suppressed without too much difficulty, and only a few of the monks made martyrs of themselves. Although Henry confiscated for his own use the jewels given to shrines, including Becket's, the bulk of the monasteries' wealth in land ownership did not stay for long in royal hands: the government had to sell most of these estates in order to finance another war against France, and thousands of new landowners became gentry with a vested interest in making this change permanent. They also gained by now possessing the incomes which the monasteries had received as 'rectors' of more than a quarter of the parishes. The other 'religious' orders, for example the Franciscans, disappeared with even less fuss.

It is often said that Henry divorced the English Church from the papacy, and closed down the monasteries which had been a central feature of medieval Church life, because of his desire to divorce the first of his six wives, Catherine of Aragon. That is true up to a point: the king was in love with Anne Boleyn, she had refused to become his mere mistress (unlike her sister), and he was already in the habit of identifying his will with the will of God. But royal marriages have seldom been contracted or ended solely for reasons of the heart. The main point in the 1520s was that the only surviving child of the marriage was a sickly girl, Mary, and the king believed that the peace of the realm depended on his having a son as his heir. This belief was shared by many of his subjects, for the Tudor monarchy seemed a better alternative to the civil wars of the previous century, and in that rough world a man stood a better chance than a woman of keeping 'the king's peace'. During many years of negotiations Henry also had a sincere (and convenient) belief that he had a case in theology, for Catherine had previously been married to his elder brother Arthur.

The young man had died before he had had sexual relations with his Spanish bride but Catherine had failed to have her virginity registered, and a law in the Old Testament had forbidden marriage to a brother's widow although another law had encouraged it. It was believed by Henry, and by most other people, that if he had the wish a pope had the power to resolve such difficulties to a prince's satisfaction. In 1491 a French king had been helped in this way, and for many years Henry trusted that his own first marriage could be declared no marriage at all (in an 'annulment', not a divorce). But Charles V, the Holy Roman Emperor and Catherine's nephew, sacked Rome in 1527 and made the pope a virtual prisoner. In the terms of practical politics this ruled out a concession to Henry.

He married Anne secretly in 1533 and had her executed publicly three years later after an allegation of adultery: she had given him no more than another daughter (Elizabeth) and he now had another interest, Jane Seymour. Thomas Cranmer, an obscure Cambridge scholar, had come to the king's attention because he advised consulting the universities about the justice of the royal wish. Now Archbishop of Canterbury, he both officiated at Anne's wedding and talked with her as her disapproving priest on her last night. It is no surprise that years later Henry died clutching this useful archbishop's hand. A more surprising fact is that to the end Henry considered himself a good Christian and a good Catholic.

Back in 1521 the king had put his name to a book defending the seven sacraments of the Catholic Church against Martin Luther's Protestant heresies, and the pope had awarded him the title 'Defender of the Faith' which English monarchs have used ever since. After the rejection of papal jurisdiction there were religious innovations but Henry made sure that these were kept to the minimum needed to take a few steps towards a more definitely English version of Catholicism. Among these steps the most important was allowing an English Bible to be sold openly. Most of it was the work of William Tyndale, who had also deployed his mastery of languages in a literary controversy with Thomas More. He had learned Hebrew in order to understand the Old Testament. For the New Testament he had depended on the Greek text recently published by the great scholar Erasmus, and had made a close study of Luther's translation into German. Forced to work abroad, Tyndale had been burned as a heretic in Belgium in 1536, but Miles Coverdale had completed and revised his work. All parish churches were ordered to buy this Bible by Easter 1539, but because they were so slow they had to be threatened with fines; anyway only members of the élite were able to read this big and expensive book privately. In 1544 Cranmer was allowed to produce a short 'litany' of prayers in English but he did not make his growing Protestantism widely known. The conservatism of the king and of most of the people was shown in the official insistence in 1538 that priests must remain unmarried and should 'offer the sacrifice' of the Mass for the benefit of the living and the dead. The Mass included the change of the 'substance' of the bread into the Body; after denying this John Lambert was given a show trial and burned. Thomas Cromwell, who had been Henry's chief agent in the whole process of the Reformation up to this point, was executed in 1540: he had served his turn.

As he grew old the once glamorous Henry became fat, diseased and at times aware that he could not control the future. At last he had a son but the boy (who became Edward VI) was too young to govern, was being educated by tutors with Protestant ideas and was to die at the age of sixteen. When the old tyrant died in January 1547 his will provided for two priests to pray for his soul at Mass until the end of the world, but before the end of that year the chantries where Masses were offered in intercession for the dead were suppressed. So were the fraternities which had arranged such Masses. These changes which affected, and bewildered, parish churches all over the country were made on the orders of a government moving rapidly in a Protestant direction.

This drastic change of policy was inspired mainly by the self-interest of the aristocrats in power. The more conservative nobles had been executed under Henry, and the newcomers were determined to get hold of the wealth of the chantries and of many of the estates owned by the bishops. They intended to keep as much as possible in their own possession but otherwise to use the proceeds as a substitute for taxation in a period when taxes were specially unpopular because of the economic distress. The Duke of Somerset, for a time Protector of the Realm, was overthrown by the Duke of Northumberland – who, however, was to follow him to defeat and execution. Thieves, it is said, fall out: so did these nobles.

In the churches, 'images' and stone altars which had been allowed under King Henry were now removed as symbols of a defeated Catholicism. In their place a Book of Common Prayer entirely in English arrived in 1549, accompanied by an Act of Uniformity. The book was a compromise between Catholic and Protestant theology but the Act insisted that there should be no more diversity in the details of the services (which had been the practice in the Middle Ages). What this implied for the future was indicated in the suppression of the elevation of the consecrated 'host' for adoration; instead, the climax was the communion of the people. And another pointer to the future was supplied by the daily services for morning and evening:

these largely consisted of recited psalms and readings from the Old and New Testaments. The Bible was to be dominant. In response there was a rebellion in the west country but in 1552 a more Protestant book was imposed by the government. Compiled largely by Cranmer, the new Prayer Book still included old prayers for the week ('collects') translated by him into beautiful English. The Mass, however, was now definitely a Communion service. Provision was made for it to be held on every Sunday and saint's day but there was to be ordinary bread, no longer a wafer changed in its 'substance' by the priest's words. With the wine, this bread was not to be offered to the Father as a sacrifice on a stone altar but was to be distributed from a table in remembrance of the 'full, perfect and sufficient sacrifice' made by Christ on the cross. Anything left over after the Communion was to be taken home by the priest for ordinary use. The clergy were ordered to 'subscribe' (agree) to a statement of Protestant doctrine in 42 'articles', and a comprehensive revision of the Church's 'canon' law was drafted. To console the clergy for having to accept this religious revolution they were officially allowed to marry: like the abolition of the traditional 'vestments' (robes), it was a signal that their status had been changed drastically.

In the universities professors imported from the mainland of Europe, and in the parishes local preachers when available, began to expound the Protestant theology which had been shaped on the mainland, particularly by John Calvin the reformer of Geneva. The shape had become much clearer and firmer since Martin Luther's original protests: Lutheranism retained features of Catholicism which were abandoned by Calvinism. To these preachers, salvation depended not on 'works' performed by the devout but on the choices made by God without regard to human merits. Those 'predestined' to enjoy heaven were then given faith and grace by God. This faith was not the recital of the Church's creed, the Lord's Prayer and 'Hail Mary, full of grace', which had been regarded in the Middle Ages as the necessary minimum. The 'faith' which made any true righteousness possible meant the heartfelt acceptance of Christ's self-sacrifice on the cross where he had paid the penalty deserved by human sin. That had been the interpretation of Christ's death taught by Archbishop Anselm in the eleventh century, but now the Protestants insisted that the true faith, with this at its heart, was best taught not by any bishop – least of all by the Bishop of Rome – but by St Paul in the Bible.

The death of Edward VI in 1553 destroyed Protestantism as the controlling force in England, much as the death of his father six years previously had destroyed English Catholicism – but in both cases, the destruction was only for the time being.

An attempt was made to transfer the crown to a Protestant, Lady Jane Grey, but public opinion rallied round Henry's daughter, Mary, not least because she had bravely persisted in her Catholicism. Most of the people had had enough of the greed of the aristocrats and of the unsettling effect inflicted by the religious changes. The abolition of the chantries and the fraternities seems to have been more unpopular than the abolition of the monasteries because families did not welcome the confiscation of endowments intended to make sure that the names of the dead were remembered. Although there was no rush to endow new chantries, the Mass, the images of the saints and the festivals of the Church were now restored in the parishes with enthusiasm, and at first most people also accepted Mary's marriage to a foreigner, Philip King of Spain. (About two thousand of the parish clergy had to be removed, however: their offence was their own marriages.) The ease with which much of medieval Catholicism returned to England was considerably assisted by the decision to let the monasteries remain closed, and to let church lands which had been sold to the laity remain with the laity unless their own consciences said otherwise (which happened very rarely). And under Cardinal Reginald Pole, who functioned as Archbishop of Canterbury from 1556, reforms were planned for the restored Church: bishops were to be hard-working pastors, parish priests were to be trained, the teaching of the laity in weekly sermons was to be based on the Bible.

Then everything went wrong. Bad harvests added to the economic distress. Mary could not get herself pregnant; a bored Philip of Spain, having alarmed the English, left the country to attend to other responsibilities; an unsuccessful war led to the loss of Calais, the last French possession of the English Crown; the martyred Protestants gave the bishops an image of cruelty, although the burnings did not take place all over the country; himself accused of heresy by his enemies around the pope, Pole was summoned from Canterbury to face the Inquisition in Rome. After a period of increasing gloom and defiant fanaticism, the cancer-ridden queen died, as did her cousin, the archbishop.

There was now, in 1558, no real alternative to crowning Mary's half-sister Elizabeth, but she faced immense dangers. She was a woman ruling men, a situation then commonly regarded as a defiance both of nature and of the Bible. An exception to the rule might be made in the case of a monarch who had no brother, but in England Mary's reign had not commended the idea and in Scotland the reign of another Mary was a complete disaster. John Knox, the great Protestant reformer of Scotland, chose this moment to sound a 'blast of the trumpet' against the 'monstrous' spectacle of a woman on the throne. And Elizabeth was Anne Boleyn's daughter, and thus in Catholic eyes a bastard. She was also a heretic, since being who she was she could not acknowledge the pope's authority.

Most of the English were still Catholic in their hearts, and their conservatism had to be appeased. The bishops and clergy who refused to serve under the new regime had to go but by Tudor standards were treated lightly. In 1559 a new Prayer Book was issued, slightly changing the book of 1552. Parishioners were to be fined if they did not appear in church when this book was used, but words revived from the book of 1549 allowed them to believe that the Communion was more than a meal in remembrance of Christ's death. The parish clergy were allowed to wear the robes of a Catholic priest, and the new bishops were consecrated as traditionally as Protestantism permitted. Elizabeth did not claim to be the 'Supreme Head' of the Church as her father and half-brother had done; she left that title to Christ and there was also a feeling that no woman should be a 'head'. But she would be the Supreme Governor. The history of England would have been very different had either her half-brother Edward or her half-sister Mary lived longer.

This policy of conciliation combined with firmness where it mattered earned a reward. The 'reformed' Church of England kept enough clergy to staff the parishes, men who had gone into exile under Mary returned to occupy key positions, and with a tension between Catholic and Protestant built into it the Church could slowly be built up as one of the nation's great institutions. There was no substantial Catholic rebellion until 1569, and then its outbreak in the conservative north was not a signal for the south to rise; even Cornwall and Devon remained quiet. The pope intended to support a revolution in his favour by his 'bull' (formal letter) of 1570 which deposed Elizabeth but his intervention came too late to save the rebels. Instead it produced thirty years when it was open to any Catholic to interpret it as a command to revolt or to invade, although in 1580 the pope explained that consciences need not be troubled before it became possible to execute his order. Elizabeth's cousin, Mary Queen of Scots, was by birth her legitimate successor and by religion a devout Catholic. She was also extremely foolish: having been compelled to flee from her own country to England, she was imprisoned for twenty years. She still encouraged plots on her behalf, with the result that she was executed in 1587. In the past, Spain had been allied with England against France, and its king, although thoroughly Catholic, had not done the bidding of any pope, but there were abortive Spanish attempts to stir up a Catholic rebellion in Ireland, and in 1588 Philip of Spain launched a large fleet, the Armada, against the heretical queen. An invasion was avoided by the skill of the smaller English ships and by 'Protestant' storms.

The acute sense of national danger under these threats of rebellion and invasion made some Catholics liable to punishment as traitors, and others painfully divided in their loyalties. What was called the 'bloody question' was put to a priest who had clearly equivocated when under interrogation or torture: what would he do if the Spanish invaded? His conscience told him that either he had to condemn himself to hell by disobedience to the pope and a death without the opportunity to be absolved by another priest, or he had to accept the terrifying doom of a traitor. Whether or not treason could be proved or confessed, the laws of 1585–93 could result in the total confiscation of the offender's property and goods as punishment for repeated absences from the parish church, or in execution if a Jesuit or a priest trained abroad: even a person sheltering such a priest incurred the death penalty. These laws were enforced only in patches but it was now a fact that being a Catholic might mean being a martyr.

In the years to come controversy was to continue about the rights and wrongs in this confrontation between Roman Catholicism and the Elizabethan government, but it can be said objectively that the pope's claim to be able to release her subjects from loyalty to this queen (the last time when any pope was to make any such claim) added to the sufferings of those of the English who still accepted his authority. It can also be said that Elizabethan England was not overwhelmed by its dangers.

The country began to prosper economically and to be 'early modern' in its flowering culture. Edmund Spenser was one of the poets who linked the cult of Elizabeth the 'Virgin Queen' with Protestantism, although the propaganda suggested that she had the merits and powers of a Catholic saint. Christopher Marlowe, a dramatist who was reputed to be an atheist and who died in a tavern brawl, wrote plays which combined the new eloquence in the English language with a theme which had been prominent in the morality of the Middle Ages: for kings or scholars, pride goes before a fall. And the greatest of all the English, William Shakespeare, used the language even more gloriously. It is beyond reasonable doubt that he was a believing member of the Church of England, although he never preached, felt no inclination to write biblical plays like those of the Middle Ages, and had all Chaucer's compassion and more. And it can be argued that the essential story of his life was an epitome of the story of Elizabethan England, in danger and triumph.

It is obviously wrong to rely on any single passage in his plays as recording his own philosophy: the characters created by his imagination spoke for themselves. But it seems possible to tell what were his basic experiences. He was a patriot: his plays reconstructed the history of England so that its climax came in the establishment of national independence and social unity under the Tudor monarchy. He loved women, although in his plays their roles had to be taken by boys: his comedies celebrated their vigour and their wit, at least in the classes which had by then the new freedom of the Renaissance. Eight golden years of creativity had their climax in the exuberant joy of *Twelfth Night* in 1601. But before that he had gone through darkness; in the early 1590s the theatres were closed for fear of the plague, he himself feared death, and he was helplessly in love with the 'dark lady' who was not his wife and never would be. He said splendidly in his sonnets 'Love's not Time's fool' – but was that true? And after 1601 the darkness returned. His plays were sometimes almost failures but they included *Hamlet*, *Othello* and *Macbeth*, probing the darkness which surrounded and overwhelmed human minds; and the utterly bleak tragedy of *King Lear* was set in a Britain which Christianity had not yet touched. However, that was not the end. His plays were full of echoes of the Bible and of the Book of Common Prayer, and one of his sonnets mentioned that he said his prayers every day, even in the dark. The rebirth of hope in his later plays, in *The Winter's Tale* and *The Tempest*, conveyed a Christian message of amazing resurrection and reconciliation although not in biblical language. The richness of his genius is inexhaustible but that seems to be the sum of the story of the spiritual journey of an Elizabethan who was buried as a respectable and comfortably rich parishioner in his parish church.

Elizabeth had no wish to antagonize her Catholic-minded subjects who remained loyal to her in politics and were willing to put in at least an occasional appearance in the parish church which was under her government. Her own religion seems to have been fairly conservative although it is hard to tell since she was essentially a Tudor whose inherited profession was monarchy. Some of her prayers were written down and have survived: they sound genuine. She preferred to see an altar with cross and candlesticks rather than a bare table, as was clear from the controversial arrangement in her own chapel, and in that Chapel Royal she protected and rewarded musicians who were Catholics and whose names are honoured in the history of Church music: Byrd, Tallis and Morley. There is a story that she insulted the wife of her first Archbishop of Canterbury (Parker) because of her rooted objection to clergy marrying and it rings true: she had sacrificed marriage – why should he not do the same? In 1566 she opened her long campaign against extreme Protestants by ordering the magistrates to enforce the command that all clergy should wear white surplices, the so-called 'Romish rags'. Ten years later she ordered the next Archbishop of Canterbury (Grindal) to suppress the 'prophesyings' in which preachers were developing their skills in the exposition of the Scriptures, and when he resisted she confined him to Lambeth Palace and to minor duties for the six years of life left to him. In her view, retaining bishops was a good link with the past but the bishops were her agents. She had little interest in their pastoral work, allowing her father's provision for 'suffragan' (assistant) bishops to lapse. Their estates were useful as enabling the bishops she appointed to live as peers of the realm. They were also valuable as an addition to her own revenue during vacancies and as a source for rewards to her courtiers.

The men she liked among the clergy combined a rejection of the pope with a strong belief in her right to control the Church. This was the attitude of John Whitgift, the disciplinarian who followed Grindal, and of Richard Bancroft, the Bishop of London who was to follow Whitgift. It was also the position of two considerable theologians, John Jewel, who defended the changes made at the beginning of her reign although he would have preferred to see them more definitely Protestant, and in the 1590s Richard Hooker. Their learned argument was that the popes had added doctrines and practices to Scripture and the purity of the early centuries: thus they could maintain that the Church of England was more truly Catholic than the Church of Rome. Indeed, popes had added so much corruption that Hooker could write: 'We disagree about the nature of the very essence of the medicine whereby Christ cureth our disease.' This was, however, not a reason why there should now be a total break with the past, and his main attack was directed at radical Protestants within the Church of England who were nicknamed 'Puritans'.

They were passionately sure that the Church still needed to be purified. They had a long list of survivals from the past to which they objected, ranging from ceremonies to Church government by monarch and bishops instead of by meetings of godly preachers. Hooker could defend these survivals theologically: Catholics who obeyed the popes in the Middle Ages or in the present were wrong to do so, but not wrong in absolutely everything, for although preaching mattered, worship (particularly the Eucharist) mattered more, and many customs inherited from the centuries of Catholicism could be aids to worship. In his own writing he set an example of not relying on the Reformers of the sixteenth century whom the Puritans venerated: he saw Christianity in a much wider setting. How, then, were the Christians of that century to judge what was truly Christian in their heritage? Hooker formulated what was to become the classic Anglican reliance on Scripture, on 'Tradition' meaning the whole inspired experience of the Church of Christ, and on reason as the God-given glory of humanity. And if this left the ordinary Christian bewildered, Hooker had a simple answer: it is the will of God that laws (the biblical laws taught or endorsed by Christ, the laws of nature and the laws of justly constituted human authorities) should be obeyed. His volumes on *The Laws of Ecclesiastical Polity* taught that the laws made by the monarch with the consent of the Parliament were in effect the laws of God for the people of England. All of them ought to be contented members of the Church of England, established by these laws.

One trouble about this theory was that no Protestant argument, no persecution and no dilemma in politics could stop some of the English from being faithful to the 'old religion'. Some of the faithful were also open to a new movement, called too negatively the 'Counter-Reformation', which was renewing Catholicism and making it more emphatically 'Roman' Catholicism, with a new emphasis on the papacy as a religious force, on the Jesuit missionaries under his command, on self-denying priests trained abroad, and on laity whose devotions were more intensely emotional, praying as the priest recited the Latin words of the Mass, made uniform by the pope in 1570. This renewal produced internal tensions, specially between the Jesuits and other priests, who criticized them because their enthusiasm exposed the whole Catholic community to the charge of treason. But without this renewal, the 'old religion' might have died as those who were nostalgic for the days when it had seemed utterly secure came to the ends of their own disappointed lives. What happened in fact was that Roman Catholic numbers shrank under Elizabeth but remained quite strong in Lancashire and could survive elsewhere if a landowner sheltered a priest, maintained a chapel, encouraged his employees, tenants and neighbours to attend, and was not much troubled by the government because he was respected locally, seemed loyal and kept quiet. And where this fire of Roman Catholic faith continued to burn in some English hearts, it could be fanned into flames.

Another trouble about Hooker's theory that the Church of England consisted of the people of England was that Puritanism was a version of Christianity with a great spiritual strength. It maintained that the Protestant Reformation needed to be completed if it was to resist the counter-pressure applied by the renewed Roman Catholicism: faith, courage and holiness must confront faith, courage and holiness. For the time being Elizabeth's government of the Church could be accepted by all except the hotheads: she had become the symbol of English patriotism, she was getting old, her successor would be a Protestant theologian, King James VI of Scotland, during whose reign Catholicism was being almost completely exterminated. But the day would come in England for what Robert Browne desired: 'Reformation without tarrying for any.'

The clear theology was adapted from the Calvinism of Geneva by English scholars such as William Ames and William Perkins, who were practical pastors not anti-government controversialists. This theology dominated the universities of Cambridge and Oxford where some four thousand licensed preachers were trained for the parishes during Elizabeth's reign. Puritanism proclaimed a call to conversion which reached the hearts of many of the most idealistic members of the new generation, and after that conversion they knew that their lives ought to be 'godly'. They took the road to heaven, with great work to do as they travelled. They were given God's grace which would ultimately prove irresistible, and food for their journey to their destiny was provided by the English Bible, read privately as the Word of God, expounded in powerful (and often long) sermons and versified in psalm-singing.

The importance of the Bible in language which the people could understand was now acknowledged by Roman Catholics, who had their own Douai Version in opposition to the Puritans' favourite translation which had been published in Geneva. But no form of

Catholicism – not the pope's and not Richard Hooker's – could match the grand simplicity of the Puritans' use of the Bible: they read it for themselves, they believed that they found in it the assurance that they had been chosen and called by God, and they were also sure that, so far from any Roman addition being needed to this infallible book of instructions, the pope was clearly mentioned in the Bible as the predicted Antichrist. It is significant that most of the leading men in Elizabeth's government and most members of her Parliaments were more Protestant than she was, whether or not they sympathized with the Puritans. Her favourite archbishop, Whitgift, was a Calvinist in his own theology, and his assistant in the campaign against the Puritans, Bancroft, was driven by their argument that the equality of the ordained (Presbyterianism) was Scriptural to insist that, on the contrary, Scripture taught that the Church needed bishops. The Church of England's official Articles of Religion were never revised after 1571: a revision which left them plainly Protestant although not exclusively Calvinist or Lutheran.

A few of the Puritans became 'separatists', refusing to use the Prayer Book or to worship alongside the ungodly, but the first substantial and long-lasting congregations in England were not formed until the 1610s. A few took refuge in the Netherlands; there a Puritan preacher, John Smith, was so convinced that his baptism as an infant had been invalid because contrary to Scripture that he baptized himself. He could not find anyone willing and suitable to do this for him, but his lonely action was a prelude to the spread of English-speaking Baptists, to number many millions, with their insistence that only believers, not infants, should be baptized. After about thirty years of more informal contacts between congregations, the first national assembly of English Baptists was held in 1654. But meanwhile the Elizabethan government had a way of reminding Protestant 'separatists' that their disobedience to the queen had connected them with the Catholic 'recusants' whom they hated: three were hanged in 1593.

When he became King of England in 1603 James remained a Protestant but refused to allow any concessions to the Puritans, insisting instead on obedience to bishops who would insist on obedience to him (and he imposed bishops on Scotland in 1610). 'No bishop, no king, no nobility' was his own summary of his warning. The one positive result of his meeting with the Puritan leaders was that 54 scholars were set to work on a revision of the English Bible of Tyndale and Coverdale and the Bishops' Bible of 1568. There was now a better understanding of the original Hebrew and Greek but most of the old English was kept, giving the 'Authorized' Version an air of old-fashioned majesty when it was published in 1611, to begin an influence which lasted for some three hundred years. Protestantism could not replace the rituals which had been effective in making the people of England Catholic but the impact of the Bible in English was now shaping minds and imaginations.

For many years it seemed possible (at least to the unrealistic) that either Puritanism or Roman Catholicism would unsettle the settlement which had established the Church of England under Elizabeth. It also seemed uncertain what would be the character of this Church which in the nineteenth century was going to be called 'Anglican'.

Under James I and his son, Charles I, who liked clergymen much more than Elizabeth had done, this Church was showered with favours. Its bishops recovered much of their prominence in the affairs of the nation and some of their wealth. In the parishes the clergy had an equivalent experience and 'canon' law, guiding them, was revised in 1604. And there was a recovery in spiritual life, not with the intensity of the Roman Catholics or the Puritans but producing great poetry from John Donne, George Herbert and Henry Vaughan. These poets did not escape into a world of dreams as (for example) Spenser had done: their style was to take the physical objects of everyday experience and to see in them clues to the infinite love of God.

Before his ordination Donne had acquired a reputation as an explicit poet of sexual love; his devotional poems, like his sermons, were now brilliantly eloquent variations of a prayer which might be summed up as 'ravish me' – before death. 'All our life is but a going out to the place of execution, to death,' he pointed out to his congregation. 'Now was there ever a man to sleep in the cart ...?' Donne was Dean of St Paul's in London, George Herbert a scholar who was for three years a parish priest. That short ministry inspired him to complete *The Temple*, a book of poetry fragrant with a love for Christ, and to write a book of practical advice for a 'parson' loving his parishioners. For him prayer was

> The milky way, the bird of Paradise,
> Church-bells beyond the stars heard, the soul's blood,
> The land of spices, something understood.

Vaughan learned the art of poetry from Donne and the aspiration of prayer from Herbert. Although he knew the misery of defeat in a civil war, as the 1640s became the 1650s,

> I saw Eternity the other night,
> Like a great Ring of pure and endless light,
> And calm as it was bright ...

In the main, however, the story of the Church of England in the first phase of the Stuart monarchy is sad to relate. Its most distinctive belief became insistence on the 'divine right of kings', meaning that having a king for a father, and becoming a king oneself, resulted in being given by God an unquestionable authority over Church and State. Although it was difficult to derive this simple belief from the Bible or from the Church's tradition, it was believed by the Stuart kings themselves – which was what mattered for practical purposes.

James I had no real policy except to be king in peace, feasting and hunting, after a terrible childhood and a difficult reign in Scotland. He did not appoint the ablest of his bishops, Lancelot Andrewes, to Canterbury: instead he chose a safe Calvinist who was archbishop for 22 years but is remembered only because he accidentally killed another man when out hunting and found being a 'man of blood' an additional handicap in Church leadership. As his successor Charles I appointed William Laud.

Laud had ideas and used the government in a doomed attempt to make England accept them. He alarmed many of the laity by giving the impression that the clergy were back on the road to power and wealth. He alarmed many of the Puritans by treating as 'orthodox' churchmen sympathetic with the Dutch theologian whose Latin name was Arminius, a heretic in the eyes of Calvinists. Arminius taught that Christ died in order to save all, not merely the 'elect' whom God had predestined to heaven, although he warned that the divine grace given to those who believed in Christ could be resisted and lost by human misconduct. Here was a division of opinion about whether few or many might be saved, and it was therefore a disagreement about the conditions and prospects of humanity. It divided the Baptist congregations into 'Particular' (Calvinist) and 'General' (Arminian). But among the Anglican Arminians the greater optimism about the human situation was combined with a belief that the pope was not Antichrist – which meant in practice that Rome needed to be reformed but some customs of the 'old religion' could be more actively maintained or revived. For Holy Communion an altar could again be used, behind a low rail at one end of the church: it looked more dignified than having a table in the centre. Beauty should be restored in the Church's buildings and services; worship was more important than hearing or half-hearing sermons. After the church service people need not stay at home for further religious exercises; manly sports such as football were not wicked on a Sunday afternoon. The Arminian idea was that people should be happy to worship, happy to relax, and happy to obey their divinely appointed king.

To Puritans such 'innovations in religion' were sinister signs that the Protestant, Bible-based identity of the Church of England was being altered – and they did not fail to notice that both James and Charles had Roman Catholic wives. James wanted friendship not war with Catholic Spain; Charles brought Rubens and his pupil Van Dyck over from Catholic Belgium to add to his fine collection of paintings. In fact neither of these kings had the slightest intention of accepting the papacy. On the contrary, because in 1605 a few Roman Catholic conspirators could not keep secret a plot to blow up Parliament, Guy Fawkes was arrested in a cellar among his barrels of gunpowder, 5 November was to be observed as a day of celebration with bonfires and cries of 'No Popery!', and persecution continued although in patches. But to the Puritans there seemed to be a great danger that kings and bishops would conspire inside the Church of England to destroy Protestantism at the very time when the hugely destructive

Thirty Years' War (1618–48) was being waged by Catholics against Protestants in Germany.

In those years the numbers of the English in regular contact with Roman Catholic priests increased to about sixty thousand, and hundreds became priests, monks or nuns, or at least Catholic exiles in France and Belgium, but in the history of the world the most important reaction to the religious situation in England was the escape of many thousands of Puritan families across the Atlantic. They went in order that they might build a 'godly commonwealth' in New England.

The Pilgrim Fathers who sailed in the *Mayflower* in 1620 were inspired by the promise of the pastor who had ministered to them in their temporary exile in the Netherlands: the Lord had 'yet more light and truth' to give them out of the Bible. Ten years later a larger group was led by John Winthrop, and that voyage was the real beginning of a systematic and successful attempt to build 'the kingdom of Christ in America', finding detailed guidance in the Bible as interpreted by Puritan preachers. In the little, vulnerable settlements which came to be called New England, an emphasis was developed from the Puritan tradition: God had made a 'covenant' (contract) with his chosen people that they would not perish, and the members of a congregation made a covenant with each other that they would live in the light of the faith which they had declared to each other before being permitted to join (and therefore to vote in elections). Until Roger Williams founded a little colony on Rhode Island there was no sign of freedom of religion: what the pioneers in Massachusetts wanted and got was freedom only for their own consciences and families to follow the light as they saw it. In the south, Virginia was already beginning to prosper as an English colony, on the basis of slave-grown tobacco and with some (not much) work by clergy of the Established Church. In New England, however, there was a new lifestyle as the Puritans did their own work and achieved moral and material results which have never been forgotten although many other ingredients have gone into the history of what would become the USA.

In the history of England the result of Puritan hostility to Arminian 'innovations in religion' was a civil war. Of course the war was not caused entirely by disagreements about theology. There were economic causes for a volcanic upheaval in society: England had again become overpopulated (one motive in the Puritans' transatlantic migration), and different social groups were rising and falling in response to the new conditions, including a degree of modernization. It was possible to respond to this social crisis by urging more regulation (by whom?) – or by daring to advocate democracy. There were constitutional issues even when the idea of democracy seemed mad, because both James and Charles disliked having their policies questioned by Parliament, and Charles attempted to rule without summoning peers and MPs to air their views before voting taxes. There was a real fear that England was falling under an unchecked despotism and this anxiety was shared by men who in the war were to take the king's side. But although no Englishman was executed for heresy after 1612 this was a century when the English people as a whole expressed its deepest feelings in religious terms and it was not complete hypocrisy for every group in the conflict to announce very loudly that it was defending the truth of the Christian Gospel. Families united by economic self-interest were divided by the mixture of religion with politics. The religious question was prominent in the relationship between England and Scotland, which often decided the course of events.

Charles I had to allow Parliament to meet in 1640 because he needed taxes for an army to put down a rebellion in Scotland. This had been sparked off by his foolish decision to impose on the Scots a Prayer Book which was not only very like the Book of Common Prayer in England but also included Catholic-looking parts which had been dropped in the English revision of 1552. It was a double insult to Scotland's nationhood and to its Calvinism. Unsurprisingly, when Parliament met it was far more interested in reversing the king's policies in England than it was in reversing the Protestantism which had become part of the national character of Scotland. Charles had to consent to the execution of his chief minister, the Earl of Strafford, and always blamed himself for this betrayal of a faithful servant. Incident after incident showed the king and the majority in the House of Commons (supported by many peers) to be at loggerheads, and in 1642 Charles raised the Royalist banner to start a civil war, the first since the Tudor victory in 1485.

In the struggle between the Royalist 'Cavaliers' (from the Spanish *cavallero*, a gallant horseman) and the Parliamentarian 'Roundheads' (so called because of their short haircuts), battles and sieges were indecisive until the emergence of Oliver Cromwell in effective command of the New Model Army, no longer an amateurish force led by peers. Cromwell had been an obscure gentleman in East Anglia, a Puritan in religion but often profoundly depressed, before he acquired military skill and self-confidence. He was never to be defeated on the field of battle and never to be dismayed by any of the crises, although towards the end of his astonishing life he was to be exhausted, and (like the equally formidable Henry VIII) was to have no clear idea about what he wished for the future. With the help of the Scots his disciplined troops gained victory over the Royalists in 1645, and then he faced two questions which for other men might have been frightening dilemmas. What was he to do about the king, who in defeat persisted in futile plots to divide his enemies? And what was he to do about his army, whose religious and social opinions were not disciplined?

In the end, on a January morning in 1649, he and his colleagues had Charles executed, joining Archbishop Laud in that dangerously dramatic form of death. The king had put himself into the hands of the Scots but had infuriated them by refusing to agree to the abolition of bishops. The Scots had sold him to the English, but even then he had managed to encourage them to invade England in support of the Royalist cause. He had offered to accept the abolition of bishops for an experimental period of three years and to surrender control of the army and navy to Parliament, but whether he would keep his promises if given liberty no one knew. Now this inept king was allowed two opportunities which meant that he would be honoured as he was remembered: at his trial he spoke about the monarchy as the guardian of the laws and thus of the people, and at his execution he spoke about his faith in heaven. But for the time being the beauty of the religion which the king had loved was wrecked. In the churches a mixture of mindless vandalism and Puritan zeal destroyed much that had survived from the Middle Ages. Customs such as celebrating Christmas were suppressed as paganism.

And in the end Cromwell acted no less decisively against the Levellers, the Ranters and the other groups of soldiers, ex-soldiers and other orators who were arguing that the whole social order, a kind of pyramid, must lose its top along with the king's head. Agitators who raised democratic shouts not heard since the Peasants' Revolt of 1381, but including some biblical quotations, achieved equality for themselves: they were shot.

What was to replace the monarchy? The urgency of this question was demonstrated intellectually when in 1651 Thomas Hobbes published *Leviathan*. Hobbes had no time for the divine right of kings or for the divine right of God; for practical purposes he was an atheist although he objected to being called that. But what he thought was a scientific study of human nature in society convinced him that since human greed is contained only by human fear, in any society there must be a sovereign: otherwise anarchy will wreck everything. (The more conventionally religious Shakespeare had thought much the same.) And if the traditional structure of society was to be preserved, how were the ideals of the Puritans to be fulfilled now that they had power?

These were questions which Oliver Cromwell could not answer because the parts of the army which remained loyal to him could not agree about any long-term policy which the country would accept. Parliament had proved too talkative: it did not suit a military regime any more than it had suited the monarchy. The House of Lords was abolished; so was the House of Commons after a series of walk-outs or expulsions involving most of its members. Cromwell ruled the Commonwealth of England, Wales, Scotland and Ireland as Lord Protector, with a council to assist him and major-generals to keep order in the regions. In effect he ruled the Commonwealth because he had conquered it. But the army would not accept him as king, no other officer had his abilities or ambitions, and a problem familiar in the history of the monarchy occurred again: he had no competent son to whom he could pass his power in reality (his son was nicknamed Tumbledown Dick). After his death power passed inevitably to the army, of which the strongest section was controlling Scotland under General Monck. These soldiers might be expected to favour the Presbyterians, whose Calvinist theology and Church organization (without bishops) were also liked by many of the civilians who had prospered in Oliver Cromwell's England. In theory, the English National Church, supported by the old incomes in the parishes, was Presbyterian.

However, Cromwell himself was not. There is no evidence that he ever consulted any clergyman before taking any action. He belonged to the streak in Puritanism which has been called Independent, except that he had no patience with the political radicalism of many independents. He might also have been called a Congregationalist, except that he never formally enrolled himself in any congregation. His personal religion was very personal, consisting largely of a trust in a firm link between him and God. Since he believed that this intimately personal relationship was always the heart of Christianity, he was against the persecution of any Christians who did not seek to overturn the regime established by his God-given victories. In the parishes many Puritan pastors operated according to their own lights: the most distinguished of them was Richard Baxter, the author of hymns still loved and of countless books and pamphlets. Some discipline was imposed on parishioners, but less than the stricter Puritans had wanted. The Book of Common Prayer was not supposed to be used in public, but it was; the Lord Protector's own daughter had a wedding which used it. In return for this degree of toleration all but one of the Anglican bishops still in England refused to ordain new priests. Thousands of Anglican clergy were ejected from the parishes and the universities but pensions gave some comfort to those who went quietly.

In order to fill the political vacuum created by Oliver Cromwell's death General Monck now summoned a Parliament whose discussions demonstrated that there was no alternative open to those who wanted stability: the legitimate king must be recalled and with him the establishment of the Church of England must be restored. That necessity did not mean a return to all the old atmosphere. During his exile Charles the king-in-waiting had become a cynic whose real interests were described as 'a leg of mutton and a whore'. When he had been restored to his father's throne his court was to set the tone of much of life in what historians have called Restoration England. In contrast with the law of the 1650s which threatened adulterers with death, his mistresses were made duchesses. His horses and dogs commanded more attention than did the earnest publications analysing the needs of the Church and State. In the new coffee houses of London the talk often turned to ridiculing the dull stupidity of orthodox religion and morality, and in less sophisticated towns and villages people enjoyed the relaxation after Puritan constraints. But there was of course another side to Restoration England, a side which was serious even if the wits laughed at it. When General Monck had been rewarded by a dukedom and the army had been paid off, when Charles II had been crowned and anointed, much of the population wished to settle down to a life in which religion and morality were honoured – although not with a Puritan strictness.

The Restoration of the monarchy in the 1660s brought triumph to the Church of England. Its experience of being the minority dissenting from a Presbyterian National Church, or of being a number of Royalist refugees exiled from their own country, had deepened its sense of its own identity. In part this was a sense of moral and spiritual strength which did not depend on political privilege. Some of its leading thinkers had published books which supplied a detailed commentary on the Church's creed and guides to 'holy living' and to 'the whole duty of Man' in every-day life. Jeremy Taylor wrote the first Life of Christ in English and did it beautifully. Other leading clergy had become all the more convinced that there was a biblically-based and dignified Anglican style of worship, neither Roman Catholic nor Puritan.

In the process of the Restoration the result was that the bishops refused to make any substantial alterations to the Prayer Book: on the contrary, they indicated a rejection of the Calvinist doctrine of predestination to heaven or hell by inserting a new note saying that baptized children who died before committing a sin were 'undoubtedly saved'. A service which could be used for the baptism of adults such as 'natives in our plantations' was introduced as the tiny beginning of the link between missionary work and the British empire overseas.

More important at the time was the new clarity of rules for English Church life. Everyone admitted to Holy Communion must have been confirmed by a bishop, or must be 'ready and desirous of being confirmed' if no bishop had made himself available. Every priest allowed to work in the Church of England must have been ordained by a bishop and must swear 'unfeigned assent and consent' to everything in the Prayer Book. Some 1,760 preachers who refused to take this oath were ejected, and the Act of Uniformity which heralded this Prayer Book of 1662 forbade anyone to teach in a school without a bishop's licence or in a university without being a member of the Church of England.

But the Anglican triumph was not unlimited. Bishops could not use the courts of High Commission and Star Chamber on which Archbishop Laud had relied in his disciplinary campaign, for these were scrapped; and the clergy had to abandon their medieval privilege of voting their taxes in their own Convocations, independently of Parliament. Above all, it was permanently clear that the land ownership which had passed out of the hands of the clergy into the grasp of the laity since 1530 (perhaps covering a quarter of England) would not return to the clergy.

In practice the parish church probably now depended more on the 'squire' (the local landowner) than on the 'parson', and the pompous tombs of squires' families might be the most conspicuous art in churches: a change from the medieval saints. The priest was often poorly paid, either because he had been appointed to one of the many parishes which were too small or because he was a 'curate' paid by a rector who, being a graduate with a family, might think himself entitled to receive the income of more than one parish and to live where a decent house was available. Most of the people in the parish accepted the Church of England – as they had to, for baptism was the only way of registering a birth, a wedding in church was the only way of making a marriage legal, and there was no alternative to being buried in the churchyard. But not all attended the Sunday services, and in most parishes only about a tenth communicated at the 'celebrations' of Holy Communion, usually four a year. That service was for the holy who (as the defeat of the Puritans had shown) were the minority. As he recorded in his diary, Ralph Josselin had to abandon hopes that the Kingdom of God would arrive on the earth of England, and to lament that the English turned to Charles II 'out of love to themselves', but he did not wear the 'popish' white surplice until he took fright in 1680. He remained the vicar of a village in Essex from 1641 to 1683, praying for the patience to accept God's mysterious decrees of sunshine or rain, health or sickness, republic or monarchy. Another country clergyman recorded thoughts which were far more beautiful and hopeful in a notebook which was bought for a few pence off a barrow in 1895. Thomas Traherne found consolation in a mysticism enjoying God in and through the Herefordshire countryside. That give him a 'felicity' which he had not found in Puritan theology or ethics, and which he did not think was on offer in the 'High Church' views of the senior clergy – but he knew that nature did not provide a complete religion, and after ten years in that village he accepted an invitation to leave his rectory for a post in London, where he did not survive for long.

He made the move in the year after the Great Fire of London which had destroyed many other medieval churches in addition to a large but decaying cathedral, 'Old St Paul's'. The reconstruction of these churches, financed out of taxes, gave his greatest opportunity to an architect of genius, Christopher Wren. He had to modify his initial ideas because of the conservatism of the clergy, but he designed the new cathedral and the new city churches (more than fifty) and they were plainly churches for the laity. The light of nature came through clear windows and no candles were needed by the congregation as it listened to a sensible preacher expounding the morality commanded by the Creator in the new St Paul's under a great dome. What was valued was what was natural and rational, legal and moral – and that was the entire universe as seen by a scientist of genius, Wren's contemporary, Isaac Newton. He was a devout believer in God who, however, filled many secret notebooks with his independent thoughts about the Bible and theology. His published work, based on experiments in Cambridge, explored the composition of white light and the force of the gravity which kept the planets in their courses and governed movements on earth with only occasional interference by the 'Lord of the Universe'. The creation of the world by God, and its subsequent control by him, could be demonstrated because without God matter would not behave in an orderly fashion; for example, the stars had originally been comets. For 24 years Newton was elected President of the Royal Society for Improving Natural Knowledge, a group of professional or amateur scientists which investigated 'things not words' under the patronage of Charles II. One Anglican bishop was its real founder, another celebrated its destruction of medieval fantasies when he wrote its early history.

The light which seemed to come from these sources to an age which was beginning to be 'the age of reason' was needed, for the Church of England was being forced to abandon what had been at the centre of its teaching: its belief in the divine right of kings. In a democratic age it seems very strange that a frequent toast at dinners was then 'Church and King!' and that it could be thought that God prohibited any resistance to a dictatorial monarch who owed his or her throne to the sole fact of his or her birth. Yet at the time it was believed that power and authority were derived from God and that the gift of a hereditary monarch 'by the grace of God' avoided civil war. Sound doctrine seemed to justify the oaths which had to be taken under the Act of Uniformity not to 'endeavour any change or alteration of government either in Church or State' and never to 'take up arms against the king on any pretence whatsoever'. This tradition of 'non-resistance' could be supported by many quotations of praises of kings in the Old Testament, and could even be called the 'doctrine of the cross' on the ground that Christ had accepted the verdict of the emperor's representative, Pontius Pilate. But the theory proved unable to cope with the realities of history.

Neither Charles II nor James II was willing to accept the old basis, which was that the Church of England taught this unquestioning obedience in exchange for the assurance that it would be treated as the sole legitimate Church in the nation. The touch of seriousness, even of sadness, which remained in Charles' character found its outlet in the conviction that the Roman Catholic Church had the only religious claims which deserved to be taken seriously. From 1661 to 1679 he was in difficulties because the 'Cavalier Parliament' combined a devotion to the memory of the Royal Martyr with a persistent refusal to vote taxes which would have met the needs, official or personal, of the current monarch. He therefore felt obliged to accept a secret, but large, annual pension from the French king, Louis XIV. He could not ignore the warning that the loyalty of his subjects was not unconditional, and he wisely postponed his formal acceptance of the Roman Catholic Church until he was on his deathbed in 1685. Because he never had a legitimate child, in the 1670s it became clear that his successor would be his brother. It also emerged that James was a deeply convinced 'Papist'. Partly because he shared the immorality of the Restoration court, he knew that he and many others needed forgiveness and instruction. Being military as well as royal in character he was a firm authoritarian, and he drew the conclusion that forgiveness and instruction in morality and religion (but not in politics) must come from the pope.

It was a problem for both Charles and James, how to protect from persecution the Roman Catholics whose faith they shared. By this time the bulk of English public opinion was totally hostile to 'Popery'. In 1678 nonsensical stories about a 'Popish Plot' to seize power by violence were believed so widely that executions of 'traitors' followed, and included the hanging of an Irish archbishop (Oliver Plunkett) whose true character was saintly. This outburst of hysteria died down, but in 1685 Louis XIV seemed to offer a fresh demonstration of the true character of Roman Catholicism by expelling all Protestants from France. His intolerance was thought to provide a good reason why Roman Catholics should be persecuted in England, and by 1715 their numbers had shrunk to about fifty thousand in a population of 5.5 million. There were not now many executions, but to fierce unpopularity had been added a pressure which seriously hit the landowners on whose patronage many of the surviving Papists relied: in law, no Roman Catholic was allowed to inherit or sell land. The main hope seemed to lie in patronage at the very top of English society – the support of a king.

The strategy of Charles and James was therefore to use their own royal authority to issue declarations of 'indulgence' suspending the operations of Parliament's laws against all 'Dissenters' although the

Protestants included in that description vastly outnumbered the Roman Catholics; in 1715 they were five times as many. This attempt failed mainly because all the emotions which had inspired the rebellion against the 'arbitrary government' of Charles I now came to the surface again, together with the fear of a revival of Popery. But another reason for the failure of the two kings' strategy was that the Protestant Dissenters refused to be identified with the Papists. They knew that their problem was persecution by Anglicans, between 1662 and 1672 and (after a confused period) between 1681 and 1687. Unless they received Holy Communion in the Church of England they were forbidden to hold 'conventicles' (meetings) for worship or to seek any office in national or local government. Their preachers were under special disabilities; their publications were censored; their sons could not graduate, and any schoolmaster needed a licence from a bishop. Fines or prison could be severe penalties for any infringement of these laws, which were enforced with zeal by many magistrates. And like the persecution of the Papists, this Anglican attack on the Protestant Dissenters did great damage. The aim had to be the conversion of the Anglicans to the cause of toleration.

The divisions which had produced the tensions between Presbyterians and Independents within the ranks of the Puritans under Cromwell could not be healed now that each congregation had to fend for itself, only loosely connected with others in a 'denomination'. For a time Richard Baxter provided intellectual leadership, as did John Owen, who had been chosen by Cromwell to lead Oxford University. But they died and no one replaced them.

The greatest spiritual force was exerted by George Fox, born humbly in a village, in his youth already extremely unconventional, who began to preach in 1647. He promised a direct experience of Christ and the Spirit, of light and power, without any reference to the Churches and with little dependence on the Bible. He proclaimed a radical simplicity and equality among his followers whom he wished to be called 'Children of the Light'; the name 'Society of Friends' emerged but their many enemies called them 'Quakers' because they could surrender themselves to ecstasies. Under Cromwell's regime they could shock people, specially because their women could speak about the Spirit's guidance (as they did in other sects, equally shocking). A Quaker leader, James Nayler, caused an outrage by riding into Bristol on a horse in imitation of Christ's entry into Jerusalem, with a mixed group crying 'holy, holy, holy' and two women leading the horse: he was punished savagely and Fox was as angry as anyone about the blasphemy. In Charles II's reign the Quakers needed all their courage to confront popular contempt and official hostility. Then William Penn, Fox's successor in the leadership but the son of an admiral and the friend of kings, became absorbed in the foundation of Pennsylvania in the land granted by Charles II in America. And in England the Friends, unable to pursue any profession, turned to trade and to banking and commerce, accepted a strict discipline, grew rich and respectable, and eventually became Christian more in behaviour than in theological belief. In the years to come Quaker spirituality was to give far more prominence to silence than to ecstasy.

The Presbyterians lost most when under persecution because the 'presbyteries', meetings of ministers which maintained Calvinist orthodoxy and strict morality, could not function. As their unity was lost and their numbers declined, many of their ministers were attracted to beliefs which could be called Unitarian because they stressed the unity of God whether or not they attributed any kind of divinity to Christ; and whether or not Unitarianism appealed, Calvinism did not, for Presbyterians were now among those who found it incredible that a good God had demanded the sacrifice of the Son in order that the few who had been predestined to heaven should be able to reach that goal.

The noblest exponent of Puritanism, the great poet John Milton, rejected Calvinism – openly in a theological book (which was, however, written in Latin and not published until 1823) and by implication in his poems *Paradise Lost*, *Paradise Regained* and *Samson Agonistes*, published 1667–71. His intention was 'to justify the ways of God to Man' and he did it by seeing God as aloof from the details of human history. According to him, a human soul was not created afresh by God: bodies and souls owed their existence to human reproduction after the creation of Adam and Eve. The Devil and his angels had rebelled against God; so had Adam and Eve, justly punished by the terrible wrath of God; but a few of the descendants of Adam and Eve, aided by God's gift to them of a conscience, could be heroically virtuous and thus be saved through a return to obedience. As they toiled 'under the great Taskmaster's eye' Jesus could help them, for this Son of God had 'God-like power'. The saints would often be heartbroken – as the Puritans had been in Milton's lifetime after their highest hopes, as the poet himself had been when he went blind and lost his beloved wife – but by submitting to the will of God, and therefore to his unsearchable wisdom, they could end up in 'calm of mind, all passion spent'.

Milton was one of the most educated men of his century. In contrast, John Bunyan earned his living as a mender of pots and kettles and a trader in small goods, walking from village to village like his father. While young he experienced tempests of religious doubt, self-condemnation and despair, as he told in his autobiography *Grace Abounding to the Chief of Sinners*. Called to the full-time service of a Dissenting congregation in Bedford, he accepted imprisonment for twelve years, with a second period to follow, rather than undertake not to preach. During these years he learned to be a writer, but not in Milton's grand style: he wrote a story about a Puritan's spiritual journey in the language of the people and in the imagery of the English countryside. *The Pilgrim's Progress*, published 1678–84, was far more warmly Christian than Milton's poetry. The central character, 'Christian', is a pilgrim not a hero, and the decisive move in his escape from the City of Destruction comes when he lays down the burden of his sins at the foot of Christ's cross. Whereas Milton had absorbed much of the culture of the Middle Ages and the Renaissance despite his Puritanism, ultimately Bunyan's religion made his pilgrim go forward alone, with the Bible as his only book, although friends can encourage him in his many temptations. One of the sources of this interpretation of Christianity was a conversation which Bunyan overheard in his troubled youth. 'Three or four poor women sitting at a door in the sun' talked about their religious experiences which had, however, been very personal to them. They had not, it seems, been ecstatically excited as were some other women who had visions and uttered prophecies. They had simply entered into a personal relationship with God in Christ. 'They spake as if joy did make them speak,' Bunyan recalled, 'as if they had found a new world.'

The Protestant Dissent which included Milton and Bunyan could not be ignored, any more than Roman Catholicism could be when its religious power converted two English kings. In 1672 Charles, and in 1687 James, issued 'declarations of indulgence' suspending laws against both kinds of dissent from the Established Church. Parliament forced Charles to retreat, and the 'No Popery!' reaction to his move led to a futile attempt to exclude James from the succession to the throne and to a more determined persecution. The accession of James was followed by the rebellion of the Duke of Monmouth, Charles's illegitimate and brainless son. But astonishingly, 'passive' resistance was now inspired by bishops of the Church of England. James had seven of them imprisoned in the Tower of London amid great publicity. There was already intense alarm about his appointments of Roman Catholics to key positions in the government and the universities. There was some genuine converts to Rome in this period; the poet John Dryden was one. But when a son was born to James's queen the leading members of Parliament decided that help should be summoned from the Netherlands. In a panic of fear that he, the queen and the child would all be killed as his father had been, James fled to France. He still hoped, and attempted, to arouse Catholic Ireland and so recover his throne, but was defeated at the battle of the Boyne in 1690. His escape from England was taken as abdication, and his daughter Mary together with her husband William were crowned jointly as the Protestant monarchs. After Mary's death in 1694 William, who was already virtually the ruler of the Netherlands, was the sole monarch of the country which had invited him – but, absorbed in his war against Louis XIV, he showed little interest in England and less in its non-Calvinist National Church.

In one of the more heroic moments in the history of the Church of England five of the seven bishops who had been sent to the Tower by James refused to take oaths of allegiance to the monarchs whom Parliament had installed in his place. They were accompanied by about four hundred parish priests as they departed into poverty and obscurity as 'non-jurors'. In Scotland, all but one of the bishops became non-jurors and a small 'Episcopal Church' survived under their leadership while the National Church became firmly Presbyterian. But in England these Anglicans who had become dissenters fared as badly as the Puritans whom their Church had persecuted in the years of the Restoration. As a sect they were full of uncertainties and disputes, and although they produced the author of a widely influential *Serious Call to a Devout and Holy Life* (William Law) they dwindled to extinction. The last of the Stuart dynasty for whom they had sacrificed so much died as a cardinal belonging to the pope's council in Rome, pensioned by the Protestant monarchy in England: nominally, he was Henry IX.

The future lay with men such as Tillotson and Tenison, two Archbishops of Canterbury who were preachers and pastors wanting to communicate a simple, mainly moral, form of Christianity, and willing to accept Parliament's verdict about the succession to the throne. If preachers of similar eloquence were not available in the parishes, lessons were taught by what could be seen in almost every Anglican church, where the Ten Commandments were painted on a board and the royal arms were set up over the door. Once again if there was an opportunity to include Puritans in the Church of England it was missed, but most of the bishops voted for the Toleration Act of 1689 which allowed Protestant Dissenters to meet for worship if they swore allegiance to the new monarchy and the acceptance of all but three of the Church of England's 39 Articles of Religion. Within ten years some 2,400 'meeting houses' had been built. These were plain halls with congregations facing a table with a pulpit above it. But the Protestant Dissenters were not given civil or social equality with the Anglicans, and towards the Roman Catholics (as towards atheists) there was no relaxation at all. Whatever may have been their personal wishes, once again their cause had been involved in national politics and they paid the price. In Ireland in particular, after the attempt of King James to raise an army for the invasion of England, it seemed all the more necessary to exclude five-sixths of the Irish from any say in the government of their own country and to insist that the Catholic peasants should pay 'tithes' from their crops for the support of the Anglican clergy.

Many of the clergy of the Church of England found the taking of oaths of loyalty to William and Mary a sufficient strain on their consciences: they could not bring themselves to accept the toleration of the Protestant Dissenters. John Locke, the principal advocate of the theory of toleration, did not reassure them when he published *The Reasonableness of Christianity* in 1695, for according to him the essence of Christianity was belief in Jesus as the Messiah sent by the Creator. To those who so believed that God 'proposed' the forgiveness of sins 'for his Son's sake, because they gave themselves up to him, to be his subjects' – and to obey the moral laws which he taught in plain language which the 'bulk of mankind' could easily understand. For Locke, reliable knowledge came from reasoning about evidence provided by the senses, unless God chose to add 'extraordinary' revelations. Most of the clergy, however, reckoned that the Christian revelation was more substantial than he was prepared to admit.

The men who had secured the downfall of James II were by now called Whigs; those who tended to regard the affair as a tragedy which might yet be put right were called Tories. (Both nicknames were given by their enemies: the original Whigs were outlaws in Scotland, the original Tories outlaws in Ireland.) During much of the reign of Anne the Whigs exercised power from their base in the House of Lords, but it was against her wishes. A genuinely devout Anglican (as her sister Mary had been), she regarded support for the Church of England as the supreme purpose of her life. As a sign of this, revenues which Henry VIII had acquired for the Crown were returned to the Church, to form 'Queen Anne's Bounty' for the support of the poorest parishes. She struggled to accept the many still-births or infant deaths which were her grief as God's punishments for her disloyalty to her father, but she believed it to be her duty to continue to occupy the throne he had abandoned. The Whigs' concerns were different: maintaining the position achieved by the 'Glorious Revolution' of 1688–89, strengthening the 'Great Britain' constituted by union with Scotland, developing agriculture and trade and supporting the Duke of Marlborough as he won British victories against France.

Could the victory of the Whigs be reversed? Most of the clergy were Tories and in their Convocations their representatives could be stirred into agitations with the cry 'the Church in danger!' With a restricted electorate, the House of Commons also had a Tory majority. An Act was passed stopping those Dissenters who took the 'test' of receiving Holy Communion in the Church of England in order to qualify as eligible for office in local and national government – only to return to their own chapels after that 'occasional conformity'. When the Schism Act closed down all schools which the bishops would not license, the persecution of Protestant Dissenters seemed to be resuming. The laws against the Catholic Dissenters remained but also in the air was the possibility of summoning James II's son, called by his enemies 'the Old Pretender', back home from France.

What had become the supremacy of Parliament had already been exercised, in the Act of Settlement in 1701. If no child of Queen Anne survived, Parliament had promised the throne to Sophia the daughter of Charles I's sister Elizabeth. Although some sixty people were more closely related to Anne, she had the merits of being reliably Protestant and of not living in France: she ruled the little German state of Hanover. But she was now forbidden to visit England. When she died (it was said, because of the shock of receiving Queen Anne's command), her heir was an unattractive son, George, who could not speak English. The Tories broke the Whigs' control of the House of Lords by creating fresh peerages, and concluded a peace with France. Under an able leader, Viscount Bolingbroke, who gained power on 27 July 1714, they seemed about to repeal the Act of Settlement. Somehow they would protect the Church of England (not that Bolingbroke cared much for it personally) from a Roman Catholic king who would owe his position to them. They made excited plans.

On 1 August Queen Anne died. The proclamation of George I as king passed without a hitch. Believing that 'the Tory party is gone', Bolingbroke fled to the little court of the Old Pretender in France although after ten years he returned to England, a broken man. As he returned he passed the bishop who had been the spokesman of the Tory clergy (Atterbury) going into exile. The recent Acts of Parliament against the Protestant Dissenters were repealed, and in 1717 the Whig government forbade the Convocation of Canterbury to transact any more business: the ban which meant that the Church of

England had no corporate voice outside Parliament was to last until 1852. Apart from the chapels attached to foreign embassies in London, Roman Catholic worship and schools remained illegal until 1791, although little action was taken to enforce this law. In 1715 a 'Jacobite' rebellion in the north, in favour of James, the Old Pretender, fizzled out. The French did not intervene and the same fate awaited the more alarming adventure thirty years later, which attempted to secure the throne for Charles the 'Young Pretender', who for a time attracted support in Scotland. For half a century the supremacy of Parliament would be the supremacy of the Whigs.

After about 185 years the dramas of the English Reformations, Protestant and Catholic, Puritan and Anglican, were over. To the end there had been examples of costly adherence to sincerely held religious convictions: one was provided by the Old Pretender, who refused to improve his prospects of being invited to occupy his father's throne by being willing to renounce his Roman Catholic faith. But to the end much in the history of these Reformations had depended on who did rule England.

5

Among Satanic Mills

Industrial England, 1715–1918

As the various forms of Christianity which had appeared since 1530 learned to tolerate each other (however reluctantly), and as the truth of Christianity itself was called into question (however slowly), it was still taken for granted that English life ought to have a basis in respect for religion if it was to have a respect for morality. As so there could be 'revival' as some Christians protested that a vague respect for religion was not enough. For a time people wanted peace and quiet after the conflicts which had achieved rival Reformations at such a great cost, but not many years passed before it was felt that the peace should be disturbed, that a grey scene needed a touch of gold, that a damp complacency needed some fire, that a spear and a sword could clear the path to some place where Jerusalem could be built again. The alternative seemed to be 'dark Satanic mills'. In the early stages of industrialization factories were often called 'mills', and Blake's image conjured up a large menace: the new machines making profits for the capitalists who owned them would, it was feared, grind many hearts and souls to dust. Iron machines would destroy all the richness of life with roots in traditionally shared myths and rituals, and with strengths in what was natural and humane.

In particular many people still felt the need to belong to a religious community, whether this was the parish church of a village or a church or chapel in an industrial city. Even when they rejected Christian beliefs in a Saviour or in a Creator, some people still needed to belong to a group of 'free-thinkers' looking somewhat like a Dissenting or Nonconformist congregation. So what Christian community would be the most successful in attracting support from a population which grew rapidly? And what would be the beliefs and values of the millions who did not belong? These questions were answered by great struggles for the soul of a people. But as the twentieth century opened, the impacts of modern lifestyles and scientific knowledge had begun to make much of English life secular, or at least unchurched, at a calm depth where no religious community seemed to possess truth or to offer life, and where no militantly secularist congregation was needed to advocate this immense change which was to be called (in Germany, by Nietzsche) the death of God.

Some of the pressure on the Churches was intellectual and it had a history behind it. When the Reformations had destroyed the security of the medieval Church as an institution there was a sequel which the defenders of the medieval faith had predicted: questions about the truth of Christianity itself were asked openly and answered negatively. The bitterness and destructiveness of the disputes about what should replace the medieval Church added to the force of the wish to forget 'revealed' religion in any shape, and even among those who remained, or became, open to claims about a revelation it was not easy to reach a simple agreement. William Blake had managed to draw inspiration from a myth about Jesus in England. But if the Bible did include myths, what kind of truth did it still teach? Or should Christians be very careful before describing any part of it as mythological?

Francis Bacon, Lord Chancellor under James I, outlined a project to move beyond *idola*, by which he meant illusions, into an accurate knowledge of nature. (He caught a fatal chill by stuffing a dead chicken with snow in order to discover the effects of refrigeration.) He, and those who followed his cautious advice, exempted the Bible from investigation: it was 'the book of God's words' while nature was 'the book of God's works'. But the rise of Protestantism meant that both books were going to be examined. In 1637 William Chillingworth discussed *The Religion of Protestants*: it was, he concluded, 'the Bible only' – but the Bible interpreted by the individual using reason.

When he was being buried, a clergyman who was sure that the Bible taught Calvinism threw a copy of his book on to his coffin, 'that thou mayest rot with thy author'. But when they read the Bible as Chillingworth had recommended, most Englishmen concluded that Calvinism was unreasonable since, as Archbishop Tillotson observed, it claimed that God predestined most of his children to hell and that was something which 'no good man could do'.

During the seventeenth century people gradually ceased to believe that events were caused by spirits good or bad, by the actions of angels, saints or demons. Women who seemed odd to their neighbours, and perhaps to themselves, were no longer believed to be witches who had made a pact with Satan in return for hurtful powers. During the disturbances of the 1640s witch-hunters were able to bring about two hundred such women to cruel deaths, but the last execution of a witch occurred in 1685. Although contemporaries would have been astonished to be told this, an intellectual movement in the middle of the century, which caused a number of unreadably vast books to be written in Cambridge, was a prelude to the thought of the future. In those tomes theologians faced the challenge of atheism and responded to it by relying not on reports about supernatural forces but on the wisdom of God 'manifest' in normal, natural events. It was still generally believed that there had been miracles in biblical times but eventually this innocent trust in what Scripture taught was attacked by reason and ridicule. If stories about interventions by angels, saints, demons and witches were all untrue, what was true in stories where God was said to have intervened? In 1696 John Toland's *Christianity not Mysterious* flatly denied that a true religion could include miracles or doctrines which could not be defended except by saying that they were mysteries 'above reason' (such as the Trinity). In 1730 Matthew Tindal's *Christianity as Old as Creation* argued that what was true in the Christian tradition was merely the 'Republication of the Religion of Nature'. This religion was called Deism. It consisted of belief in the Creator since the creation seemed to have been well enough designed; of agreement with the Creator's wish that people should behave well; and of very little else. It is not wholly unfair to say that the Deists pictured God as an engineer now in retirement.

At each stage of this battle orthodox Christians accused the innovators of 'atheism' or at least of spreading opinions which would end up in the denial of the existence of God and therefore in the rejection of all traditional morality. But in 1736 Joseph Butler made a calmer reply in his book on *The Analogy of Religion, Natural and Revealed, to the Constitution and Cause of Nature*. He took it for proved that there is an intelligent 'Author of nature and natural Governor of the world', but he argued that nothing apart from the sheer existence of God could be demonstrated if religion was to be confined to the contemplation of nature. 'Conscience' by itself taught nothing except that our lives must have 'a reference, of one sort or another, to a much larger plan of things'. God's self-disclosure was needed to make possible a knowledge of his character and plan – and the revelation of God conveyed by Christianity should be accepted after considering 'all the evidence taken together'. The truth of this revelation cannot be proved but then many things which are important to us cannot be proved, since 'probability is the very guide of life'. And Butler pointed out that like much in 'Revelation', much in the 'Religion of Nature' could not be proved to be true either.

This left the individual or society free to choose (within limits decreed by the State), and Butler's line of argument seemed sensible to many in the eighteenth century. He complained that in his time Christianity had become a 'principal subject of mirth' among people who were sure that it had been discovered to be 'fictitious', but in fact his book was well received. Some of the most formidable intellectuals of the age thought that if their faith was indeed 'fictitious' then the only reasonable conclusion to be drawn was despair. They chose to have faith.

Jonathan Swift, a clergyman brilliantly clever and exceptionally troubled in mind, mocked humanity's feeble efforts to be rational, including the disputes of the theologians, which he compared with wars over which end of a boiled egg should be cracked. Satire directed against human pride marked a book which as a story became a favourite with children who did not understand its implications, *Gulliver's Travels* (1726). In other fiercely indignant writing he attacked the injustice which he saw all around him in Dublin, where he was the dean of one of the two Anglican cathedrals. But in another piece of satire he produced an *Argument against Abolishing Christianity*: its abolition would result in 'inconveniences'. For Swift, one inconvenience would be the unleashing of wickedness: 'we need religion as we need our dinner'.

A layman, Samuel Johnson, was also by nature a sceptic and a pessimist. When he walked to London in 1737 after a youth of poverty and a physical disability, it was to seek an escape through the work of writing and the distraction of talk with his fellow men in taverns – talk which was immortalized in his biography by James Boswell. But he, too, feared that the end of Christianity would mean a new dark age in the world and blackness in the human spirit. He wrote prayers which show that religion was his answer to his question:

Must helpless Man, in Ignorance sedate,
Roll darkling down the Torrent of his Fate?

Fashionable people without the personal anxieties of Swift or Johnson could also think it wise to avoid being atheists, or at least to avoid being so in public. The truth of Christianity might be probable or improbable, but what could be known was that the Church was Established. In his letters to his illegitimate son teaching how a gentleman ought to behave, the Earl of Chesterfield gave advice to that effect. A far more serious and important philosopher, David Hume, did not wish his full thoughts about religion to be published until after his death, and even then they were presented in the shape of a dialogue between a sceptic (himself), a Christian and a Deist. Earlier declarations of a devastating scepticism had lost him friends, he had no wish to cause further offence, and anyway he did not believe that 'Reason' should be allowed too great a place in daily life, for 'Reason' could disturb many pleasant and useful conventions. No sensible person could believe in miracles; it would take a miracle to persuade anyone intelligent to hold the Christian faith; but he was not going to lead an anti-Christian crusade. He turned from philosophy to write a history of England, which he did not finish because on the proceeds he had grown, as he put it, 'too old, too fat, too lazy and too rich'. It seems that his real attitude was that religion could safely be left to wither away.

For people with minds more ordinary than those of the men just mentioned, the question about religion was usually answered much more simply. Christianity was not thought untrue but it was thought to be most useful when it encouraged a reasonable kind of morality. Although himself a Roman Catholic, Alexander Pope expressed this attitude famously:

For modes of faith let graceless zealots fight,
He can't be wrong whose life is in the right.
In Faith and Hope the world will disagree
But all mankind's concern is Charity.

George Frederick Handel was a Christian believer with a Lutheran background but in comparison with much music in that background, particularly J.S. Bach's, his work conveyed a sense of well-being rather than of deep devotion. His *Messiah*, composed in three weeks of 1741, was a glorious celebration of the Bible which has been widely loved, but in it the voice of the Messiah was not heard. This was mainly because the 'oratorio' was intended to be an 'elegant' entertainment for performance in a concert hall bringing benefit to a charity, and Handel had to avoid any accusation of blasphemy, but it was also the case that (as Blake was to point out) the official religion of England was not very closely connected with the religion of Jesus. Handel, whose first love was for the composition of Italian operas before he had to acknowledge that they could not make money in London, put his genius into anthems for the coronation of George II and into cheerful oratorios with Old Testament themes: there the English felt comfortable.

The religion available in the parishes of the Established Church was unlikely to disturb the peace. A representative spokesman was Bishop William Warburton, who wrote a book of the 1730s defending the 'alliance' between the State and the Church of England, established by the State because it was the largest and more useful body teaching the religious basis of morality. In a sermon Warburton claimed that 'the Church, like the Ark of Noah, is worth saving; not for the sake of the unclean beasts and vermin that almost filled it ... but for the little corner of rationality that was as much distressed by the stink within as by the tempest without.' At its most attractive, parish life was recorded in literature by Thomas Gray's poem about the peace amid the graves in a country churchyard or by the novels of Jane Austen about the emotions of the daughters of the gentry with clergymen in the background able to preside at their happy weddings; she was herself a country clergyman's daughter and was devout. The influence of the Church made for a sense of the solemnity and dignity of life and death. But the way in which the clergy themselves treated the Church was no advertisement for it as the spiritual society waging the 'Mental Fight' which Blake advocated, and it seems likely that most of the parishioners, of every class, accepted the Church more as one of the country's institutions than as a society to which they adhered through personal conviction. The normal service attended would be Morning Prayer or Mattins, which was not an occasion requiring much involvement except by the village band which might provide some music. The seating of the congregation in pews would normally be arranged according to their positions in society. People who could not afford to pay for seats could stand.

The life of the Established Church perpetuated many of the failings of the Middle Ages although most of the medieval Catholic faith and its rituals had been abandoned. Whether or not they were dutiful in holding a 'visitation' to gather information from their parishes every three years, and in ordaining clergy and confirming the young, bishops were expected to be in London for half the year: their votes were needed by the government in the House of Lords. Only in the 1840s was it agreed that there should be no more than 26 bishops in the Lords, so that it became somewhat easier to have more bishops at work in the Church. Although the population of England and Wales grew from about five million in 1700 to almost eighteen million in 1850, until 1818 it needed an Act of Parliament to create a new parish. By that date the industrial towns of the Midlands and the North were becoming overcrowded but most of the clergy remained in the old cities or the countryside – and in the countryside, too, there were problems. Although improvements in agriculture and industrial developments doubled or trebled the value of the tithes meant to support the clergy, many of the parishes could not produce an adequate 'living' (income) or provide an adequate 'parsonage' (house), partly because ideas of what were adequate were also improving. The average number of people in a parish was a mere five hundred. Only four out of every ten parishes had an 'incumbent' who 'resided', and many of the others did not even have a 'curate' who took services in the incumbent's absence. The underworld of the Church consisted of curates who had little hope of being given a parish of their own.

According to their lights most clergymen were not immoral or idle: they were expected to take two services every Sunday and to be amateur doctors and welfare workers. In the 1830s a quarter of the active magistrates were also clergymen. Some of the clergy were scholars, since about half of the young men who matriculated in England's two universities were ordained. The clergy, who remained mostly Tory, resisted the extremists among the Whig-appointed bishops who would have made the Church little but an echo of the opinions of their political masters – which was the surrender advocated by Bishop Hoadly, interpreting Christ's decision not to have a kingdom in this world. The two ablest of the bishops, Wake and Gibson, refused to make this surrender, for good or ill (one of their objections was to a plan to end the law which compelled Quakers to pay tithes to the Anglican clergy): they were therefore in the end excluded from the making of decisions. But all the best-paid jobs in the Church were in the gift of the government or of other lay patrons, and there were always candidates who would give no trouble. So ambitious clergy humiliated themselves in their scramble for favour and 'preferment'. The outcome was that the Church as an institution was not changed as the Whigs or the Tories wished: it was not changed at all.

The atmosphere in Dissent, Catholic or Protestant, was more truly impressive despite – or because of – the much smaller numbers. In a time when Roman Catholicism might seem to be dying out in England, in deepest reality it was being renewed. There were no more hopes of political supremacy; landowners were heavily taxed and their sons were excluded from the professions. Instead there was a simplification of Catholic practice, with an emphasis on morality not 'images' and on patriotism not 'popery'. The public normally respected the freedom to worship in the simply furnished chapels which were owned by lay trustees. In 1778 the government responded by allowing laymen to inherit or sell estates, and priests to function unharmed if they swore an oath of political loyalty: this Catholic Relief Act produced riots in London but it was not repealed. Bishop Richard Challoner lived to see that change after half a century of saintly work, mainly among the London poor. His unemotional teaching about regular prayer and a good life was summed up in his *Garden of the Soul*, but when he said Mass it was never in a garden: it was often in a tavern, with the doors locked.

The Protestant Dissenters took advantage of the toleration granted in 1690 but, paradoxically, declined in numbers as they relaxed. By 1720 they seem to have had about 1,200 congregations of which 350 were Baptists. Most of them preferred to get on with practical tasks in the improvement of the world and of their own economic positions, under God's eye which noted slackness or sin. Their spokesman, Daniel Defoe, published in 1724 the journal of a tour which recorded how this improvement was going ahead all over the country. Five years previously he had written *Robinson Crusoe*: in real life Timothy Cruso was a Dissenting preacher, and on the island of the story the shipwrecked sailor not only exercised his practical skills but also instructed a basically noble savage in the Protestant religion. This best-seller was followed by a novel showing how even a 'fallen' woman such as Moll Flanders could become respectable and prosperous. By the middle of the century the Dissenters were influential in many towns: it had become unthinkable to execute against them such laws as remained.

Among more prosperous and educated Dissenters the tendency became known as 'Rational Dissent'. It was fed by the Dissenting Academies, colleges which provided an education more modern than anything in Oxford or Cambridge. Whether or not it was formally Unitarian, openly rejecting the doctrine of the Trinity, it was critical of much traditional orthodoxy. Its most distinguished exponent, Joseph Priestley, was a brilliant pioneer in a number of sciences but in the 1790s he had to escape from his chapel and laboratory in Birmingham to America because of his unpopularity.

There was also a more emotional and more energetic kind of Dissent which became known as 'Evangelical' and which in the end prevailed. Its most influential figure was the hymn-writer Isaac Watts who died in 1748. Previously psalms had been sung during normal services, usually in a crude 'metrical' version. Few emotions had been aroused. Now Watts enabled congregations to share his devotion to 'God, our help in ages past', to the divine love which from the cross 'demands my all', to Jesus who 'shall reign where'er the sun …'.

In 1792 a pamphlet was published whose obscure author was William Carey, a shoemaker's apprentice who had been given a pittance (but no training) to function as a Baptist preacher. It was *An Enquiry into the Obligation of Christians to use Means for the Conversion of the Heathen*. Carey had been reading Captain James Cook's narrative of voyages to Australia and the South Pacific islands alongside his Bible and had surprised other Baptists (who had been content to believe that few were predestined to heaven) by asking: 'Was not the command given to the Apostles to teach all nations?' Ten years later he went as one of the first missionaries to India. There he developed unexpected powers as a scholar in the study of Indian languages and literature, but in this early period of missionary work most of the men and women who responded to the call were people with practical skills which they hoped would commend the Gospel to the 'natives'. Often they were disappointed but in the islands of the South Pacific they had a surprising success. In the nineteenth century English missionaries driven by a simple desire to share the blessings of their own religion and civilization scattered into many parts of the world. Hudson Taylor, for example, led a mission which preached an Evangelical message to the Chinese. Other pioneers built up church life where people of their own race had settled – in Canada, for example, or Australia. In Africa David Livingstone's skills were as an explorer; he founded no congregations or schools but hoped that he was opening up territory which others could cultivate and his death in 1873 was to be one of the events which inspired many, including many ordained graduates, to follow in his steps – often not noticing that they trod on the feelings of the 'natives'.

This missionary movement attempting to establish the reign of Jesus wherever the sun shone would have been inconceivable without a missionary movement within the England of the eighteenth century. This movement almost entirely ignored the intellectual attacks on Christianity as it almost entirely ignored the Church of England's division of the country into parishes. The two key figures were George Whitefield and John Wesley.

Whitefield had had to learn how to amuse the louts to whom he served beer in the tavern kept by his widowed mother and had been despised by the Oxford undergraduates on whom he waited; Wesley had been bullied in a more religious way, by a domineering father and mother in a rectory. After unhappiness which was increased by self-absorption and priggishness, they both experienced a 'new birth', Whitefield in 1735, Wesley three years later. They felt themselves to be flooded by Another's strength, by a love given to them, by the 'joy of heaven to earth come down'. They need no longer struggle: they had only to surrender and to depend on the righteousness of the Saviour and the power of the Holy Spirit. After this, they resolved not to be tied to the system of parishes under bishops. They would in effect be their own bishops and would preach the Gospel of the 'new birth' wherever they could, if necessary in the open air, if necessary by publicly offering prayers not in the Book of Common Prayer.

Whitefield crossed the Atlantic thirteen times and was the most influential preacher in the 'Great Awakening' which transformed religion in the American colonies. He was also tireless as a preacher in England, and when not enough pulpits were open to him he arranged for Selina, Countess of Huntingdon, to organize a 'connection', a network of chapels immune from Anglican restrictions. John Wesley was another preacher who could arouse intense excitement, but his main gift was as a methodical organizer. Although as inexhaustible as Whitefield in his missionary journeys (it was reckoned that he travelled the distance to the moon), towards the end of his life he refused to go where he would not be allowed to organize. Those who responded to his message were gathered into 'classes' for mutual encouragement and correction. He supplied them with preachers whom he controlled and with literature which he wrote or edited, not confining himself to religious topics. Much of his reading was done on horseback.

Another difference between the two men was that in the terms of seventeenth-century conflicts Whitefield was a Calvinist who believed in the predestination of the saved and Wesley was an Arminian who believed in the will of God to save all and in the ability of God to give those who responded to the Gospel 'perfection' before their deaths. But the importance of this theological difference should not be exaggerated. When Whitefield preached he hoped to convert whoever would listen, and after preaching Wesley was a strict disciplinarian in the cause of 'scriptural holiness', the 'life of God in the soul of Man'. And both men were so sure that 'God is with us' that they were not dismayed when the Anglican bishops hesitated or drew back or when mobs attacked their gatherings. In practice the most important difference between the two was that John Wesley, being more masterful as a leader, became determined that Wesleyan 'Methodism' should survive his death, whereas Whitefield preached that heaven was not interested in any division into organized denominations: the only thing that mattered was the 'new birth'.

From 1744 Wesley summoned an annual conference of the preachers whom he invited; at first, most of them were poorly paid laymen. His brother Charles (the equal or superior of Isaac Watts as a hymn-writer, with an output of about 6,500 hymns) begged him not to split from the Church of England, but in 1784 a crisis was brought about by the need for preachers to lead the Methodists in America and by the refusal of the Bishop of London to ordain them. John Wesley undertook the responsibility himself and gradually after his death Methodism became a denomination: in 1795 its 'travelling preachers' were authorized to hold their own Communion services. It was successful on a large scale in the USA. In England it was at first reluctant to be identified with 'Dissent' but then became the largest part of the expanding movement which from the 1840s was generally called 'Nonconformity'.

Towards the end of his life in 1791 the abuse which Wesley had often encountered in the early years of his mission was not the main response: many praised him – even the coldly rational Joseph Priestley, even the *Gentleman's Magazine*. Of course the praise was not universal. David Hume feared that the spread of 'superstition' would mean 'the fall of philosophy and the decay of taste'. He was writing to Edward Gibbon, who after a youthful flirtation with 'superstition' in the shape of Roman Catholicism had been impressed by the scepticism in the philosophy which Hume did allow to be published and had followed him into the writing of history. His magnificent lament over *The Decline and Fall of the Roman Empire* had one theme that the empire had grown too big, but another was that 'barbarism and religion' had triumphed over rational civilization. The first theme interested a Britain which faced rebellion in the American colonies but the second implied a criticism of a change in the fashionable culture which began in the 1760s and had triumphed by the time of Gibbon's death three years after Wesley's. People got bored with the sense of 'reason' and preferred 'sensibility'. Now the interest was in nature not elegance, energy not order, sincerity not politeness, emotions not materialism, the sublime not the commonplace. In design the severity of 'classical' restraint ceased to be fashionable: customers preferred the more romantic style which could be called 'Gothic'. (It was a revival of the Middle Ages, mistakenly connected with the energetic barbarians called Goths.) And this new mood influenced religion, so that George III was not isolated in being devout and moral, unlike the previous Hanoverian kings.

But there was not merely a change in fashionable feelings and designs. The growth in the population was both substantial and worrying. More people survived into adulthood because more food was being grown, and England was making money as the world's first industrial nation, but conditions could be grim both in the over-populated countryside and in the new factories whose owners needed 'hands' to handle the machines. It was assumed that the capitalists on whose enterprise 'progress' seemed to depend would go bankrupt if wages rose above the bare minimum and that any helpful inter-ference by the State was inconceivable. Clever clergymen were among the contemporaries who accepted these harsh 'laws of eco-nomics' as the laws of God. In 1798 one of them, Thomas Malthus, published an *Essay on Population* in which he predicted that the growth would bring doom unless people had fewer children, which seemed to him unlikely.

This new population was ignorant and therefore seemed prone to immorality and even to revolution. In 1780 a Gloucester business-man, Robert Raikes, paid four women to teach a few of the children of the poor on a Sunday, the only day when they would not be earning a few pennies: it was the beginning of the vast 'Sunday School' movement which was to keep religion alive in the working class. Some 'charity schools' already existed for children who were not at work, but more than thirty years passed before the National Society for Promoting the Education of the Poor in the Principles of the Established Church began to encourage a large number of parishes to start their own schools: it received a government grant in 1833. Another way of instructing the poor was for Bible Societies to distribute copies of the Scriptures, and many 'tracts' (pamphlets) attempted to edify those who could read.

The biggest shocks to English complacency came from the fact that the successful rebellion of the American colonies was followed by the French Revolution, in which a king, a queen and much of the aristocracy were guillotined and the Catholic Church was replaced by the godless worship of 'Reason'. The dramatic changes which began in Paris in 1789 did not end until 1815; nor did the war which was led, financed and won by England against France. And a long-lasting result was that many of the English turned back to a heartfelt religion with a conservative content. This religious revival could no longer be despised and dismissed as unreasonable 'enthusiasm'. Like Lord Nelson's navy or the Duke of Wellington's army, it had power.

Much of the reaction was conservative in a crudely and harshly political sense. John Wesley was among those who condemned the rebellion in the American colonies, and during the long war against France any movement which could be suspected as revolutionary was suppressed as unpatriotic (as 'popery' had been in earlier generations). William Blake was arrested as an agitator who might be a revolutionary because he had a quarrel with a soldier, although when tried he was acquitted because the jury in Sussex thought him strange but harmless. The Whigs lost power until the 1830s, and during and after the war there were many more serious incidents which showed the Tory government's determination to suppress publications such as Tom Paine's two revolutionary books *The Rights of Man* and *The Age of Reason*. Some rioters were shot. As late as 1834 six agricultural labourers who attempted to form a trade union in Tolpuddle in Dorset were transported to Australia as convicts. But new ideas were undeniably in the air. The classic of anti-revolutionary rhetoric was Edmund Burke's *Reflections on the Revolution in France* and Burke was not a complete reactionary: he had criticized the colonialism of the British in America, Ireland and India. His essential point was that the difficult possibility of 'virtue' demanded self-discipline which in its turn needed religion, a religion supported by a quietly developing state in a quietly developing society. Such a vision of society as a partnership of many generations and many classes could include a recognition of the need to make definite although limited reforms, intended to satisfy consciences and to increase stability.

One such reform was the abolition first of the transatlantic trade in slaves (in 1807) and then of slavery itself wherever British law ruled (in 1833). The long campaign was led by William Wilberforce in the House of Commons (from 1787) and by other committed Christians who gathered evidence about the cruelties and stirred up the nation's conscience. These men supported other reforms but to them the iniquity of slavery in the sugar-growing colonies in the Caribbean seemed the most urgent target if Britain was indeed to be Christian.

They were mostly Evangelicals, belonging to a group in the Church of England which shared the emphasis of Whitefield and Wesley on the 'new birth' but which remained attracted to the Established Church. For years this group was small and struggling. The most influential clergyman who belonged to it, John Newton, had himself been engaged in the slave trade before he had recognized the necessary consequences of his religious conversion. Two hymns which he wrote summed up his new life: he had found 'amazing grace' for himself as a sinner and then 'glorious things' in the Church of the converted as a model to society. The spiritual and moral power in Evangelicals such as Wilberforce and Newton was needed to end the production of sugar by slaves, an industry which was declining in economic importance but which was stoutly and lengthily defended by the 'plantation' owners and the merchants who made the profits. Awakened consciences were decisive in ending this evil.

Almost all Englishmen who had gone to India had gone for a simple purpose: to make money. In 1600 Queen Elizabeth had awarded a charter to the East India Company with this one aim in view, and since then the servants of the company had traded and had expanded the territory they controlled: the word 'loot' came with much solid wealth from a sub-continent where the Mogul empire was decaying. But Evangelicals did more than anyone else to change British attitudes. One who became chairman of the company wrote about cruel customs which spoiled India; another who became Governor General declared that every Indian had 'a claim upon one'; and in 1813, under Evangelical influence, Parliament insisted that the company should 'promote the interests and happiness of the native inhabitants'. This change of policy involved, as the Act said, 'the introduction among them of useful knowledge and of religious and moral improvements'. It was patronizing and the lack of respect for Indian customs was to produce the 'Indian Mutiny' in the 1850s, with atrocities on both sides – but it was better than looting.

Other reforms were accepted as necessary by Tory politicians against fierce opposition from highly placed people including the king. These Tory reformers saw that it was folly to be hostile to any group of English Christians when all should share in the struggle against revolutionary atheism. Their chief concern was to support the Church of England: they secured Parliament's approval for considerable grants to build new churches and for new laws which began to end the scandal of thousands of parishes being left without a resident clergyman. But they reluctantly acknowledged the need to include in the political system of the time Dissenters, Catholic or Protestant, excluded by outdated laws. In 1828 came 'Catholic emancipation': now Roman Catholics were at last free to vote in elections, to sit in what had become in 1800 the Parliament of the United Kingdom of Great Britain and Ireland, and to hold almost any 'office under the Crown'. The main motive was to include the Irish in the political process, but it was seen that in England also Roman Catholics needed to be taken more seriously. Their numbers were growing (partly through the influence of refugees from revolutionary France and more largely through Irish migration) and their religious claims were being asserted vigorously (for example, by John Milner, one of the bishops who were 'vicars apostolic' appointed by Rome). And in the 1830s the spirit of revival began to have a public expression: a brilliant architect, Augustus Pugin, began the nineteenth century's 'Gothic revival' by building Roman Catholic churches in the medieval style which he insisted was the only Christian architecture.

In 1829 the Test and Corporation Acts, surviving from the seventeenth century but not regularly enforced, were repealed. It could no longer be maintained that Protestant Dissenters ought to receive Holy Communion in the Church of England before taking their places in such national and local government as existed. About a third of the adult population was identified with one branch or another of dissent from the Established Church, and it was admitted that their religion was helping to make them peaceful and reliable citizens.

At this point the courage of the Tory reformers faltered: it seemed too dangerous to change any further the basis on which the House of Commons was elected, for that basis protected the rights of owners of property and in particular of the influence of the great landowners who could control elections in the 'pocket boroughs', constituencies with very few electors. Almost all the Church of England bishops were among the peers who threw out a Reform Bill introduced by the Whigs in October 1831. Riots followed and civil war seemed possible, so that most of the bishops reluctantly joined the Tories in accepting an Act which allowed about a fifth of adult English men (but no women) to vote in future elections. This Reform Act of 1832 was followed by changes in local government which increased the influence of the Dissenters, who were now allowed to record marriages and births with a registrar appointed by the State instead of having to ask the Anglican parish priest to marry and baptize. Dissenters were often still liable to pay a 'rate' for the repair of a parish church (until 1868) and had to accept the Anglican service when buried in the parish's churchyard (until 1880) but the reform of Parliamentary elections in the 1830s was also followed by a change in the system of tithes.

Non-Anglicans still had to pay a tenth of their produce as 'tithes' to the clergy of their parishes but there were to be fewer disputes because payment was to be made in cash depending on the price of the crops not on the productivity of the land. In 1891 the responsibility for tithes, which by then had almost halved in value, was transferred from tenants to landlords, further reducing arguments, and in the next century the whole system was abandoned after single payments of cash.

The Tories, who were temporarily back in power under the enlightened leadership of Sir Robert Peel, tackled the overdue task of reforming the organization of the Church of England. A commission was appointed by Parliament to inquire into the Church's revenues and duties, and its report led to the appointment of bishops and laymen as permanent 'Ecclesiastical Commissioners'. Relying on the authority of the state, this new body transferred resources from the richer bishoprics and cathedrals to the poorer parishes, mostly in the new industrial towns. These reforms of 1835–40 came too late to reverse the lead which Methodism and 'Old Dissent' now enjoyed in the competition for the religious allegiance of the new centres of population, but they were enough to make sure that the Church of England was not going to be swept away with the rest of the 'Old Corruption'. They inaugurated half a century of revival in Anglican life: the number of parishes was doubled; the number of clergy grew by almost two-thirds; many tens of thousands of 'church workers', paid or voluntary, increased contacts with the people; churches were built in the Gothic style, or 'restored' or 'improved', without number; organizations even more numerous catered for devotional, charitable, educational or recreational needs. Three hundred years after the Reformation ordered by Henry VIII, the Established Church began to have the vigour and the means to replace the popularity of the religion practised in the medieval parishes.

This legislation between 1825 and 1835 marked a shift in opinion about the role of religion in English life. The efforts to impose one form of the Church on the whole people had clearly failed but there was a new recognition of what a sincerely religious spirit, the strong morality it produced, and the voluntary membership of a religious community, could contribute. Earnest religion could benefit a society very different from the one which had been sought (in vain) by the French revolutionaries: it could inspire an England which would be mainly Anglican but not exclusively so, and mainly traditional but not inflexibly so. Here was a vision also very different from the calculations about 'utility' and 'happiness' recommended by philosophers to whom religious feelings and ideals meant little, and the turning to the 'religion of the heart' could be seen in the lives of two poets.

Looking for freedom, love and glory after an orphaned childhood, William Wordsworth thought he had discovered them in revolutionary France. Deeply disillusioned about politics and unable to marry the French mother of his child, he turned to nature. Rejecting everything artificial in life or poetry, he recovered some joy in observing and describing the Lake District, from the mountain to the flower, and in learning virtue from simple people who lived in poverty close to nature. The poems which he wrote far from France or London were to elevate and heal many spirits in the coming age of industrial uglification, with their intuition of a something, a presence

> Whose dwelling is the light of setting suns,
> And the round ocean and the living air,
> And the blue sky, and in the mind of man;
> A motion and a spirit, that impels
> All thinking things, all objects of all thoughts,
> And rolls through all things.

But his heart was broken afresh when his brother was drowned in 1805. Now he asked the deepest of questions, whether nature has any care for the individual, whether what 'rolls' also crushes. The answer which he reached was to believe firmly in a God above as well as within nature – the transcendent, saving God whom he began to worship regularly in his parish church.

His friend and fellow poet, Samuel Coleridge, made a similar pilgrimage through revolutionary politics and a mystic's communion with the divine 'All' in nature to commitment to the faith of the Church of England. He had no patience with continuing attempts to demonstrate the existence of God and the truth of Christianity by arguments based on a selective admiration for nature and on a superficial understanding of religion as a support for conventional morality. (William Paley, a widely admired Anglican clergyman and author, had claimed that the world was designed by a good God as obviously as a watch was the work of a watchmaker – and he had gone on to recommend Christian morality as eminently sensible.) Coleridge insisted that 'Christianity is not a Theory, or a Speculation, but a *Life*; – not a *Philosophy* of Life, but a Living Process ... *TRY IT*'. And nothing else in English life was so important. 'Religion, true or false,' he wrote, 'is and ever has been the centre of gravity in a realm to which all other things must and will accommodate themselves.'

During most of the reign of Queen Victoria, 1837–1901, what Coleridge said could be taken as a fairly accurate description of England, then the world's most prosperous and powerful nation. In 1876 she assumed the title of Empress of India and the imperial self-confidence which blazed like fireworks around her Diamond Jubilee in 1897 corresponded with many (although not all) realities. Gross national income doubled between the 1840s and the 1890s, as did the size of the population, and the value of Britain's exports to its empire and elsewhere quadrupled. This was the 'mother country' of an empire which was to cover a quarter of the globe and to rule a quarter of humankind, with its power sustained by some brutal force but also by the assurance that what it spread (in 'darkest Africa', for example) was peace, justice and 'Christian civilization'. Europe was mostly at peace, trying to catch up with Britain's progress, and Victoria was the grandmother of the emperors of Germany and Russia.

She meant what she had said as a girl when told how close she was to the throne: 'I will be good.' In practice she could not always be good: she was wilful when young, heartbroken when widowed, and selfishly hidden from her people in her middle years. She was not in sympathy with the Catholic side of the Church of England: she preferred the more definitely Protestant Church of Scotland, and on being told she ought not to be a communicant in both Churches she confined her participation in the sacrament to when she was north of the Border (as she often was). Her own understanding of the heart of

Christianity was, however, shared by the many English Victorians who loved hymns such as 'There is a green hill' (written in order to explain Good Friday to a sick child) and 'Abide with me' (written by a clergyman who knew that his own death was near). The emotionalism of such hymns was unashamed. Equally strong was the hope that Christ's own death would bring light to a Christian's.

So Victoria became a symbol of the stability which went with 'respectability'. It became quite common in the more prosperous households for family prayers to be held each morning or evening, with the father reading from the Bible and any children or servants lined up. Many women in the upper and middle classes did a great deal of charitable work, although if they ventured too far they could face opposition from the conventional, as Elizabeth Fry the Quaker did when visiting and changing prisons over thirty years from 1813, or as Florence Nightingale the unconventional Anglican did when beginning modern nursing for the casualties of the Crimean War, or as Josephine Butler (a priest's wife) did when campaigning against women being compulsorily inspected for venereal disease while the men walked free to have further pleasures. A stable and happy family life sustained by prayer was the theme of the (Anglican) Mothers' Union founded in a Hampshire rectory in 1876. As the middle classes grew and larger numbers aspired to their lifestyle, new organizations such as the Young Men's Christian Association (YMCA) (which began in 1844 in the bedroom of George Williams, an apprentice in a London drapery business) offered access to 'a better life' through religion. People such as clerks, shop assistants or domestic maids joined their 'betters' in the habit of regular churchgoing.

To many manual workers and their families such a habit was unthinkable: they did not possess the necessary beliefs or morals, education or energy, clothes or cash to rent pews (as was often necessary). But working-class people might go to a church if they happened to have formed a connection with one and they usually regarded themselves as Christians, 'as good as those who go'. They believed in God as Father and in Jesus as Teacher, they often sent their children to Sunday School, and they might sing hymns on a Sunday evening, perhaps drinking cocoa, as a family. If they were married (not everyone in a relationship was) it would usually be in a church. Everyone wanted a Christian burial. Of course not everyone was holy: Queen Victoria's own son and heir was what was called 'fast' in behaviour (he was an overweight adulterer with a thin mind), and city streets could be full of prostitutes. Some crooks ran companies while others burgled houses, and beer could offer an escape from poverty as gin had done in the previous century. But it meant something that in the middle years of this century Sunday was 'special' even for those who would not spend any of the day in a church.

Some of the leading politicians perpetuated the worldliness of Sir Robert Walpole and many of the other pre-1760 Whigs. Lord Melbourne, who tutored the young queen in politics, did. So did Lord Palmerston, Prime Minister for most of 1855–65. But Palmerston left the appointment of bishops to Lord Shaftesbury, whose wife was almost certainly his illegitimate daughter; and Shaftesbury not only produced nineteen hard-working (if dull) pastors as bishops but also was in his own right the greatest leader of crusades to help those who were being crushed in a society which year by year grew richer.

His childhood had been made miserable by his cold and neglectful parents, and it was sympathy with the wretched which in 1833 made this young Tory aristocrat agree to sponsor a Bill to restrict working hours in the factories to ten hours a day for adults; children were limited to six and a half. He lost his seat in the Commons partly because of the scandal caused by this proposal (and the Tory MP who had started the idea also lost his) but eventually, in 1847, the law was passed and Shaftesbury proceeded to a life which earned him the name of the Working Man's Friend. Either by pressing for legislation or by chairing a committee to organize action, or by taking action himself, he befriended the 'ragged' children of the streets, the men, women and children in the mines or in the 'gangs' which were ill-paid for work on the farms, the many poor people who had to live in squalid lodging houses, the lunatics, the blind, the cripples, the destitute incurables – in addition to his unresting work for explicitly religious causes. He was kept going by a conservatively Evangelical (and loudly Protestant) faith, and he was only one of a very large number of Evangelicals who steadily devoted themselves to the service of God and their neighbours. Even people who have rejected their creed have seen their value. As one such (F. R. Leavis, the literary critic) wrote about another (George Eliot, the name used by Mary Anne Evans as a novelist), from an Evangelical background could come 'a profound seriousness of the kind that is the first condition of real intelligence'. In *Middlemarch*, a novel of the 1870s, a dry old clergyman with a head full of useless knowledge about myths, fills the reader with indignation that Dorothea Brooke should have been so naïve as to marry him – but Dorothea herself is a woman with an increasingly independent mind and with spiritual grandeur, determined to 'do good'.

William Ewart Gladstone resembled Shaftesbury in being a completely convinced Christian ready to take courageous action, in public and private, to help the oppressed. Even while Prime Minister he gave up many evenings in attempts to 'rescue' prostitutes from that extreme of exploitation: this activity seems to have finally persuaded Queen Victoria to believe the accusation of his arch-rival in politics, Disraeli, that his speeches full of lofty idealism were utter hypocrisy. But unlike Shaftesbury, Gladstone was primarily a statesman – and was that well into his eighties. In the 1860s he took over from Palmerston the leadership of the Liberal Party formed by a coalition of the old Whigs and the new radicals. In some ways he was never a radical: he remained a convinced believer in the claim of the Church of England to be the Catholic Church of the country, fully entitled to teach it religion. Since Nonconformity was more or less identified with the Liberal Party in politics, that meant that no demand for the Church's disestablishment would be successful while he was the Liberals' leader. But in other ways he changed radically from the days when he had been described as the 'rising hope of those stern, unbending Tories' – and he changed because of his Christian conscience.

'I was brought up to distrust and dislike liberty,' he told John Morley who would write his biography. 'I learned to believe in it. That is the key to all my changes.' That conversion brought him into conflict with the Tories, now aptly called Conservatives since they sought to defend as much as could be defended of the old social order, in particular looking after the interests of the landowners and the Established Church, while also meeting some of the demands of the new industrial work-force for the sake of society's stability. As Chancellor of the Exchequer under Palmerston, Gladstone thought it his moral duty to give liberty to the businessmen who were making Victorian England prosperous, removing barriers to international trade and reforming taxation so that it no longer subsidized the inefficient or discouraged the enterprising. This belief in small but efficient government helps to explain why so much good work was left to charities such as those led by Shaftesbury, but Gladstone was called the 'People's William', convinced that 'free trade' and liberty for industry and commerce would in the long run benefit all the people – as indeed happened. Having missed the opportunity to widen the electorate by including the more respectable of working men in the towns (a reform achieved by Disraeli in 1867), he gave votes to the agricultural labourers in 1884. He refused to share Disraeli's imperialism, concentrating his eloquence instead on denunciations of the Turkish empire. And his boldest moves were made in the interests of the Irish people at a time when English and Anglican dominance over the whole of that island were usually thought to be essential to England's greatness. In 1870 it was enacted that the Irish dioceses in the United Church of England and Ireland should be stripped of their privileges and much of their wealth. In 1886 Gladstone did his utmost to secure 'Home Rule' for Ireland, with a Parliament in Dublin deciding many matters, and he renewed the attempt when back as Prime Minister in 1892. By that policy he split his own party (as his hero Robert Peel had done in 1846, when in order to make food cheaper for the poor he had repealed the laws protecting the Tory farmers from foreign competition). On the second occasion he was forced to retire from the political arena.

One of the paradoxes of the Victorian age was that although Gladstone was its greatest Anglican – indeed, its greatest Englishman – the bulk of the Church of England was Tory or 'Conservative'. The true explanation is not that clergy or churchgoers were all criminally indifferent to the sufferings of the poor. No doubt there were sinners of that kind and one factor was the continuing influence of the landowners; in this age just over three-quarters of the land came to be owned by some seven thousand families. The Conservative Party was for the most part inspired by the privileged (such as the clergy), most of its financial support came from traditional sources of wealth (such as land-owning) rather than from new forms of industry and commerce, and the people were expected to be grateful for charity, not impatient for justice. Yet a Christian sense of duty towards the 'less fortunate' was undeniably strong in Victorian Conservatism. Many of the laity felt it. Many of the clergy pleaded for the improvement of living conditions; for example, they contributed to the pressure which brought about the Public Health Act of 1848. Particularly towards the end of the century, they organized an elaborate network of 'missions' and charities. But much evidence suggests that the workers, the unemployed and their families used the churches rather than feeling that they belonged to them: they provided an audience in the church and received charity outside it.

Even the small band of Anglican idealists known as Christian Socialists avoided political Socialism when they responded sympathetically to the Chartist disturbances in 1848 (when a radical 'People's Charter' listed demands). Amid fears of a revolution in London they urged patience on the discontented and understanding on the powerful, and they had practical plans for a Working Men's College and for 'Co-operatives' in which workers could combine instead of being mere employees. These experiments were tried but of course dismissed by Karl Marx as 'holy water' sprinkled on the real problems, and the most influential outcome was the theology of F. D. Maurice. He advocated co-operation rather than competition because to him all England, and humanity as a whole, should be seen as fundamentally united as a family, created by the one Father, saved by the one Son who was now King of all, inspired by the one Spirit. To Maurice the baptism of an infant was essentially a declaration that he or she was already a child of God; the Church's worship was 'the speech and music of humanity'; the Church's buildings were signs that 'the city and the men in it are holy'. Before his death this prophet spoke to his son of many disappointments but made a summary which contrasted with Gladstone's praise of liberty: 'The desire for unity and the search for unity, both in the nation and in the Church, has haunted me all my days.'

When Bishop George Selwyn returned to England in 1854 after thirteen years spent planting the Anglican Church in New Zealand, he commented on a 'great and visible' change during his absence. 'It is now a very rare thing to see a careless clergyman, a neglected parish or a desecrated church.' The Victorian Church was united in its energy although being energetic it was also argumentative. Colleges were at last founded to train parish priests for their work. Most of those ordained were graduates and in the ancient universities the teaching to some undergraduates of traditional theology using more-or-less modern methods of study was at last attempted (in the 1870s). Elected representatives of the clergy met in the revived Convocations of Canterbury and York. Their proceedings were not decisive, since one change made in the 1830s was the transfer of jurisdiction in the most important cases affecting the Church to bishops and laymen sitting as the Judicial Committee of the Privy Council. This body seemed set to interpret ecclesiastical law as making for a fairly 'liberal' (meaning liberty-loving) interpretation of the Protestant Reformation. A clergyman who denied that the baptism of an infant guaranteed a spiritual rebirth (which could be lost by later sin) was upheld against his bishop who insisted on the power of this sacrament. Other clergymen who published *Essays and Reviews* in order to welcome modern approaches to the Bible were upheld against thirteen thousand of their brethren who signed a declaration of belief in the Bible's divine inspiration 'without reserve or qualification'.

This liberal Protestant or 'Broad Church' position was taken by A. C. Tait, appointed in 1868 to be the most active Archbishop of Canterbury for more than a hundred years, and gradually opinion in the Church moved to the attitude that the more conservative Evangelicals were better at preaching and working than at thinking. In the 1860s 'revivalist' campaigns began, often around preachers from America, and it was possible to applaud them as a second Evangelical 'awakening'. But the term 'revival' was significant: the appeal of the preachers with their accompanying musicians was to revive a simple and stoutly traditional faith. The impact on the public was limited, as was the impact on the average Anglican. Similarly, quieter conferences (at Keswick in the Lake District supremely) revived a sense of personal consecration among those who already believed. There was in England no new huge and loud-mouthed movement comparable with American fundamentalism.

In the Church of England a definite alternative to the 'Low Church' Evangelicals was provided by a reinvigorated 'High Church' movement. This treasured the Catholic emphasis which had never been entirely lost in Anglicanism but which before this energetic age could be called merely conservative, 'high and dry'. Many people whose early life had been influenced by Evangelicals with the permanent result of religious 'seriousness' came to regard that creed as too narrow: Gladstone was one. They might find their ways into a wider heritage: the faith and life of the Catholic Church through the ages, particularly its worship, centred on the Holy Communion which was now often called by its old names, the Eucharist and the Mass. Even when Morning Prayer or Mattins was still the main service of the Sunday for the middle classes, with Evensong often attracting larger and less affluent congregations, the worship was more dignified than it had been, with robed choirs and good organs and with hymns such as those collected in *Hymns Ancient and Modern* (1861). There was a new emphasis on the importance of bishops, not as peers of the realm but as the apostles' successors: and on the Church led by bishops as a society with its own strong tradition, a body with a touch of glory, which in relation to the world around ought to be a model not a servant. Tait's successor at Canterbury, Benson, set up his own court which ignored the Privy Council and made some practices in 'Catholic ritualism' legal in the Church's eyes, and two Bishops of Durham who had been Cambridge professors embodied the Church's recovered confidence. Lightfoot was an historian who proudly traced continuity with the early centuries, Westcott a scholar who took part in the preparation of a more accurate Greek text on which a revised English version of the Bible could be based. He was also a visionary who claimed for the Church the moral leadership of the nineteenth century. While bishops, both men made an impression on the (mainly Methodist) miners and on the other manual workers, to the extent that Westcott was asked to act as mediator in a miners' strike. At Easter in 1911 the Church of England had a million more communicants than at Easter in 1881. In the same period other Anglican statistics, most notably the numbers of men being ordained, began to decline, but this particular rise showed that the existing clergy had persuaded many of the laity that Holy Communion was necessary because it fed the Church and could be a sign to society.

What gripped the imagination of many was the thought that the Church was now spread around the world. One hymn for evening use said what had never been said before:

> As o'er each continent and island
>   The dawn leads on another day,
> The voice of prayer is never silent,
>   Nor dies the strain of praise away.

And the hope grew which another hymn, marching into a new day, celebrated with a boundless confidence:

> Nearer and nearer draws the time, the time that shall surely be,
> When the earth shall be filled with the glory of God as the waters
>   cover the sea.

However, as Anglican missionaries got to work in all the continents, inevitably they took somewhat different paths. In South Africa, for example, there was a conflict between Robert Gray, the 'High Church' Bishop of Cape Town, and John Colenso, the 'Broad Church' Bishop of Natal, who caused a stir by writing against the complete accuracy of the Old Testament (he was a mathematician by training and the Zulus asked him to be honest). The bishops of 'the Church of England in Canada' (as it was called) were so concerned about this dispute that they brought pressure on what they called the Mother Country. And so the Archbishop of Canterbury was persuaded to convene the first international 'Lambeth Conference' of Anglican bishops, which met in 1868. But the tensions continued.

In England they became acute as a result of the Oxford Movement, so called because in 1833 three 'fellows' (teachers) of colleges in Oxford University began to urge other priests that they owed their authority to Christ and his apostles, not to the State. They were called Tractarians because they issued *Tracts for the Times*. John Keble denounced what has seemed to most people a perfectly sensible act, given the situation, for the government reduced the number of expensive posts in Ireland's Established Church, which being Anglican was rejected by nine-tenths of the population. The point for Keble was that this was the State trespassing into the Church's territory, which he loved with his whole being: essentially a country priest, he wrote simple and tenderly beautiful poetry about *The Christian Year*. Later the most learned of the Oxford Movement's three founders, Edward Bouverie Pusey, influenced an energetic recovery of conservatism in the Church. Traditional doctrines inspired traditional holiness and self-sacrifice; traditional architecture, hymns and rituals created a more devotional atmosphere in church; Anglican nuns and monks appeared; this great tradition was brought to the slums despite some Protestant riots. But it was John Henry Newman who aroused the most interest, even before he made his courageous decision that since its bishops would not accept his Catholic interpretation of the Church of England's official documents (as those who had written those documents would not have done) he must become a Roman Catholic.

He became one in 1845 and about 450 Anglican clergy made the same move. After that blow, leaders such as Keble and Pusey rallied many to be loyal both to Catholicism and to Anglicanism and that double loyalty gradually replaced the Evangelicals at the centre of the Church of England's life. In 1874 Parliament foolishly passed a Public Worship Regulation Act in order to suppress what thorough Protestants attacked as 'Anglo-Catholic ritual', but after a few imprisonments of priests it was seen that the law could not be enforced and early in the next century it was admitted that the Book of Common Prayer needed to be revised. However, despite this strong Catholic tendency within Anglicanism it remained a question whether Newman had not been correct in seeing the logic of the Oxford Movement. And there was a further question: did he have something to contribute to Rome?

Newman never wavered in his belief that he had been right to obey his conscience and therefore to accept the authority of the papacy as the Catholic Church's divinely commissioned centre of orthodoxy and unity. But it was also the case that he never felt entirely at home in the Church he had joined. Partly this was because the pope was Pius IX, whose conservatism was more extreme than his own. When in 1870 the First Vatican Council taught that the pope was 'infallible' (incapable of error) when teaching *ex cathedra* (with a special solemnity) on matters of faith or morals, Newman accepted the doctrine but was not enthusiastic about its new definition. Most of the Roman Catholic bishops in England shared this position. But when that 'hierarchy' had been restored in 1850 its members had been appointed by the pope and at their head the flamboyant Cardinal Wiseman had been almost more Roman than Rome. Initially Wiseman was so foolish as to announce that he had been sent to 'govern' certain counties but he quickly recovered ground by declaring that his real aim was to care for the poor, for example in Westminster's slums. As his successor in the archbishopric of Westminster (1865–92) the pope had appointed Henry Manning, like Newman a convert from Anglicanism but unlike him a thorough 'Ultramontane', meaning that the Catholic seeking truth should always look for it to the south beyond the mountains (the Alps). Newman taught, more cautiously, that doctrine could and should develop within limits but that before new definitions were decreed as 'dogmas' essential to the Catholic faith the faithful ought to be consulted.

At this point he had a further problem because in England most of the faithful Roman Catholics raised little or no objection to the authority of a priest, bishop or pope. This was partly because most of them were Irish who accepted the clergy as community leaders. In the first half of the nineteenth century numbers increased from about 100,000 to about 750,000, large families maintained the growth in the second half, and for most of the faithful the decisive event of the 1840s was not Newman's conversion but the blight caused by plant-pests which ruined the potato crops on which Ireland had depended. The famine caused the death or emigration of about a quarter of the population. Many of the refugees went to England's new industrial cities, particularly to London and Liverpool, Manchester and Birmingham, where there was already a considerable Irish settlement. At first they were destitute and ready to accept any work at any wages; often they could not speak English; and often coming from a countryside where

Catholic priests were rare and Anglican clergy bitterly unpopular, their religion was not church-centred. Although almost all the bishops were English, this influx of the Irish overwhelmed the Catholicism which had become 'polite' in an eighteenth-century style, with its priests called 'Mister' and its laity often dependent upon landlords.

Now missionary priests from Catholic countries were recruited to join a campaign which needed all the energy of the new century. It was a campaign to build churches and schools with the pennies of the poor, collected Sunday by Sunday; to excite a more decided faith by a more fervent preaching; to popularize the devotions to the 'sacred heart' of Jesus, to his continuing presence in his Body in the 'blessed sacrament' reserved for adoration in the golden tabernacle, to his 'immaculate' (sinless) mother using the beads of the rosary to suggest prayers. The response of many of the English was to add hostility to the initial alarm and contempt (specially in Liverpool). But eventually the Irish could be admired for their hard work and strong family life, and although by no means all of the Irish attended Mass every Sunday (it might be easier to find the men in the pub) the influence of the Church in this transformation was decisive. Priests and people together built up a community so united in discipline that when artificial contraceptives began to be available and the Church taught that they went against nature and should not be used, the ban was generally accepted even within the beds of the married. Births could be controlled within the enjoyment of marital sex only by reliance on the 'safe period' in the month – and there was a safe period in the discussion of the Church's doctrines, for the usual attitude (even among the well educated) was a simple acceptance not needing argument. This was the community's triumph, celebrated early in the next century under Cardinal Vaughan by the building of a great new cathedral in what had been a slum area of Westminster, and by Archbishop Richard Downey's planning of an even larger cathedral to overlook the port of Liverpool. But the second great church was never built above ground level: the triumph did, after all, depend on priests and people who never became rich materially.

Many differences from the Church of England worked out to the advantage of the Roman Catholic community in the nineteenth century (whether or not Pope Leo XIII was right to condemn Anglican ordinations as 'absolutely null and utterly void' in 1896). The twelve bishops – men such as Ullathorne, in Birmingham 1850–88 – looked more obviously apostolic; they did not live in large houses or vote in the House of Lords but their authority over the faithful was unquestioned. These bishops were not involved in controversial politics; they made sure that the faithful did not arouse hostility by becoming revolutionary, and in the struggles between the parties in Parliament their sympathies were divided, for Gladstonian Liberals were favourable to the Irish cause yet the Conservatives could be looked to more hopefully for support for church schools.

Partly because they had no middle-class families to support, Roman Catholic priests could be poor among the poor and always available. While now powerless in relation to their bishops, in relation to their parishioners they had a very great power for they regularly heard their most intimate secrets in the confessional and their guidance was asked. And boys and girls were likely to be deeply influenced by the Church. In the boys' schools set up by the Benedictines and Jesuits the fees for an excellent education were lower than those in the snobbish Anglican public schools. In the Anglican Church there were now nuns but they were suspect as being not sufficiently Protestant; in contrast, the Roman Catholics loved their nuns while they respected their priests. In addition to the many parish schools at the primary stage, there were fee-paying schools where these 'sisters' made a special contribution to the education of girls: among them were Cornelia Connelly and Laura Jerningham, who between them founded a network of 'convent' schools and the great Catholic Training College for teachers in Liverpool. Cardinal Manning had been shrewd to insist on the building of schools before money was spent on conspicuous architecture, as he had been shrewd to be far more active than any Anglican bishop in the expression of sympathy with working-class discontents. These two policies made the Roman Catholic Church part of the working-class culture, to an extent impossible for the Anglicans and for most of the Nonconformists. In the industrial cities of the Midlands and the North, where the Church of England was at its weakest, this community was strong: in the 1910s more than half of all Roman

Catholics in the country lived in the ecclesiastical province of Liverpool. But of course the Mass was where the Church came together. Despite the Evangelical and Catholic revivals Anglican worship was still usually sober if not dull, while in Roman Catholic churches the use of Latin and incense added to the sense of drama and mystery. Even when no service was being held the Body of Christ was always there to be 'visited' and the doors were open to the poor.

Perhaps only in one field did other Christians have an obvious advantage over these Roman Catholics: the others could pursue religious truth with more freedom. During the nineteenth century the issue was not prominent but in the early years of the twentieth a crisis came. By then most of the community was marked by the Ultramontane enthusiasm of converts or by the sense of deference to the clergy in the Irish and the other working-class faithful but a small group of scholars explored modern knowledge and thought. Under Pius X Rome now conducted a campaign against 'modernism' and demanded from all who claimed to be Catholic teachers an oath of complete faith in traditional doctrine. Out of loyalty to the Church a number of scholars ceased to work on problems in biblical studies (for example). Baron von Hügel, who was sheltered from the storm by being a lay aristocrat, persevered in some independence but wisely concentrated on the history of mysticism and spirituality. Edmund Bishop became so learned in the history of Christian worship that he made clear its early simplicity and thus encouraged what became the 'liturgical' movement to involve the people in the action of the Mass. The writer who suffered most was a Jesuit, George Tyrrell, who when he accused the papacy of 'medievalism' was excommunicated. The Church also suffered, for until the 1960s those of the English who took an interest in religious questions could often regard Roman Catholic teachers as spokesmen rather than independent thinkers. This did not mean that such teachers had no influence, however, for some of them were highly gifted as communicators.

Very different was the atmosphere in Nonconformist worship – less formal than the Anglican services, but also less dramatic and colourful than the Roman Catholic Mass and less disciplined than the Roman Catholic community. The secret of Nonconformity was that its worship could arouse in people, individual by individual, a simple trust in God as Father and in Christ as Saviour. That was the message preached in the sermons and sung in the hymns, and the extempore prayers suggested the appropriate response in terms of daily life. In practice if an inadequate preacher was in charge the service could be as dull as anything in an Anglican church, but even if the preacher failed, around the worship there could be a 'fellowship' which was 'bright'.

These were two of the Nonconformists' favourite words and the words were not empty. Almost the whole of the community could be included in the fellowship of a Primitive Methodist chapel in a mining village, finding some precious brightness in a life otherwise absorbed in domestic drudgery for the women and danger and poverty for the men. Even when a parish church kept much of its old role the chapel could be the place that was loved because it was intimate, as when a Lincolnshire villager told an Anglican priest that they went to the church in the morning 'to please you, sir' and in the evening to the chapel 'to save our souls'. And even in what seemed to be an industrial city without a community or a soul, some Nonconformist chapel might gather a group which could make it a home, whether it was in a little 'Bethel' in a back street or an example of Wesleyan Methodism's 'mahogany age' seating the affluent. Thus 'fellowship' and 'brightness' were offered to Nonconformists who sat under a pulpit no less than to Roman Catholics who knelt around an altar.

Activities were organized for many groups, from the Sunday School to the old folk, and people who were glad to get out of their houses were specially grateful to the chapel for giving them these opportunities for enjoyment and 'improvement'. And beyond these activities, which often had lay leadership, even leadership by women, Nonconformity thought of itself as a whole culture, as a movement which had purified Christianity as the old Puritans had wished but which had done so in a way which was popular, so that there was every prospect it would be able to purify the nation's life as well. Whether or not they were as smug as their critics (specially novelists) alleged, these Victorian Christians knew that they could offer what many people wanted. In 1851 the first (and last) official census taken of church attendance on a Sunday suggested that 44 per cent of those at worship in any church were Nonconformists: about 20 per cent Methodists, a tenth Congregationalists and 8 per cent Baptists. The Anglicans had only 7 per cent more in their churches: this was less than a quarter of the population and only a third of those who thought of themselves as 'Church of England'. The Nonconformists had some seventeen thousand places of worship compared with the Established Church's fourteen thousand, although they had only half the number of seats in comparison with the Anglican churches.

Towards the end of the century confidence in the mission of the 'Free' Churches (as Nonconformity was now increasingly called) reached a new height. It was an age of great preachers (who, of course, were not typical). A Methodist leader, Hugh Price Hughes, inspired the building of a 'Central Hall' in every major city: with an orchestra, chairs, specially powerful sermons and specially bright social activities, it deliberately did not look like a traditional church. As a preacher he had such influence that he ended hopes of 'Home Rule' for Ireland when he denounced the Irish leader, Parnell, who had been cited as an adulterer in a divorce case: 'what is morally wrong can never be politically right.' Together with the spread of the 'temperance' movement which fought the trade of the brewers by campaigning for total abstinence, this protest which unintentionally postponed Home Rule was the supreme example of the Nonconformist Conscience in action. In 1892 Hughes inaugurated the Free Church Congress, proclaiming that 'the future of British Christianity and of the British empire is in our hands'. National and local councils kept this spirit alive and many other preachers deserved to be called princes of the pulpit. In Birmingham R.W. Dale influenced not only the Congregationalists gathered under him on a Sunday but also the whole of the movement to make a modern, clean and educated city under the Liberals' local government. On a Sunday in 1886 in south London about ten thousand people heard a more conservative Baptist preacher, Charles Spurgeon, in his 'tabernacle', and on a Sunday in 1903 about seven thousand heard Joseph Parker in the 'temple' in the midst of the City of London. The explosions of Parker's oratory could echo around England: 'God damn the Sultan!' was heard in Turkey.

In 1906 no fewer than 185 men with a Nonconformist background were elected to Parliament, and four years later a distinguished preacher who joined them, Charles Sylvester Horne, declared that 'there is no church meeting that is more constantly and practically concerned with living religious problems than the House of Commons'. Here was the heady atmosphere of a crusade within sight of Jerusalem.

But even if we end this chapter's story a mere dozen years after 1906 we have to observe that the crusade did not lead to victory. On the contrary, the statistics of Nonconformity began to decline.

The failure to achieve the disestablishment of the Church of England was not the most significant of the disappointments, since one reason for it was that the Established Church's privileges were greatly reduced during this century – although always against opposition from many or most of the Anglican clergy. From 1853 onwards the Liberation Society, a pressure group for disestablishment, employed agents to influence the constituencies before either of the main political parties, but the 1880s had arrived before the House of Commons included a really influential number of men who had definitely separated themselves from what that society called the 'State Church'. By then the remaining Anglican privileges in England did not seem so obviously evil or unpopular that a government must give priority to their time-consuming abolition. In Wales, which was predominantly Nonconformist, the situation was different, although even in Wales disestablishment was not effected before 1920 (after legislation secured in 1914). There was a great contrast with France, where in 1905 Church and State were separated as enemies, with an emphatically secular school system to shape the future of the Republic. In England Nonconformity had no wish to attack traditional Christianity: on the contrary its complaint was that the Established Church was not Christian enough and not sufficiently energetic in the rejection of whatever was morally wrong in the nation's life.

One problem was that despite the lessening of discrimination against it Nonconformity could never match the Church of England's influence over the education which produced leadership and prestige. Most of the great names in Victorian industry and commerce were the names of Nonconformists for whom (as for Daniel Defoe) improvement in the economy went hand in hand with improvement in religion and morality. But the children of enterprising capitalists had many temptations to lapse into Anglicanism: for example, in the first half of the century higher education was virtually an Anglican monopoly. Moreover, Nonconformists had to admit that there was no real hope of financing enough schools for the 'lower' classes to rival those controlled by the Church of England. When the day of compulsory education came at last they had to accept the Board Schools of 1870 which taught the Bible but not any 'denominational' belief. In the end they also had to accept the decision of a Conservative government in 1902 to subsidize Church schools (Anglican and Roman Catholic) more generously, although there were many strong protests and some who refused to pay their share of the tax through local 'rates' were imprisoned. It had to be admitted that many parents wanted such schools for their children and that the State did not want to replace them by increasing taxation still further. In the 1940s about half the schools in the nation were still Church schools.

The chapels themselves provided millions of people with education in a broad sense, not only in the spread of information and appreciation through the sermons and the social activities but also in the cultivation of the arts of speech and influence – arts which could be exercised in political agitation. But despite all the idealism in the pulpit what became known as the Nonconformist Conscience did not produce a positive and practical programme for politics, or a great political leader. John Bright, a Quaker who was the first Nonconformist to belong to a cabinet (in the Liberal government of 1868), was not a crusader but a Lancashire businessman who had a conscience but was prepared to disagree with any preacher. Much later it seemed that another Liberal government was creating a society which would be truly democratic, and its leaders, Asquith and Lloyd George, paid attention to the Nonconformist Conscience: yet neither really believed in orthodox Christianity or in married faithfulness.

Above all, working-class Nonconformists could refuse to vote for the Liberalism which some of their employers supported. In the 1890s Methodists such as Arthur Henderson were among the chief architects of the Independent Labour Party. Economic problems had now intensified because British agriculture could no longer compete with cheap imports from North America, Australia and New Zealand, and the new, technically advanced, industries of Germany were outstripping British industry, which had relied on its export of manufactured goods to the empire and to other countries which had been largely without even the simplest of machines. Imperialism was one answer and Joseph Chamberlain, a Unitarian who might have been Gladstone's successor as the Liberal leader and the Nonconformists' hero, in fact took his political machine in Birmingham, and many of the more prosperous Nonconformists elsewhere, into alliance with the Conservatives. His 'Unionism' defended the union with the whole of Ireland and advocated the protection of trade within the empire by building walls of tariffs against all foreign competition. But this empire-building answer was not very convincing in terms of economics, and the early years of the twentieth century saw the trade unions making moves and threats, and gaining numbers and privileges, which made the replacement of Liberalism by Labour very likely.

To many people Nonconformity's denunciations of sin seemed too negative in a way which mattered as much as this inability to mobilize a positive and united political movement coping with economic questions, for people who were not happily involved in 'chapel life' could think it dreary, unintelligent, insensitive and life-destroying. Matthew Arnold delivered a famous attack on it as 'Philistine', meaning uncouth and unenlightened: he was not fair to the huge educational activity of the chapels, and sounded like the superior Anglican which he was, but novelists who had more in common with Nonconformity told a similar tale. Above all, Charles Dickens, who more than anyone else spoke about, and for, the middle and working classes, and as a radical could have been expected to identify himself as a Nonconformist, avoided commitment to any congregation. He wrote a *Life of Christ* for his children; his novels praised Christian virtues and domestic happiness; but he had Shakespeare's contempt for Puritans. It is true that he did not practise what he preached about family life: he deserted his wife and blamed her in public. But his defence of humanity against those who reckoned themselves to be holy, as well as against its ruthless exploiters, was not entirely discredited by his restless life. In return for the dedication of his genius to this humane cause, he was widely loved and he destroyed his health by giving too many public 'readings' from his novels for he needed contact with his public. His life, like that of the far less sentimental George Eliot, was shaped by emotions and values which in the next century were to be called 'post-Christian'.

Another weakness of 'Nonconformity' was its disunity. Even when that name, which seemed to make a religion out of disagreement, fell out of fashion, the 'Free' Churches remained divided. In the nine-teenth century the Unitarians and the Quakers ceased to grow in numbers and many of them ceased to be firmly Christian in belief although even the orthodox could admire their lives. The Congrega-tionalists and Baptists were increasingly torn apart by disagreement about the authority of the Bible; thus Spurgeon walked out of the Baptist Union because he maintained that it 'downgraded' Scripture, and Parker was followed in the pulpit of the City Temple by R.J. Campbell who preached a 'new theology' until he himself saw through it. And even Methodism, which its founder left safely in the hands of the conference of invited preachers ('the living Wesley'), could not contain in one fellowship the tensions produced by class divisions. In the early years of this century various groups whose emphasis was far more lay and far more radical rebelled against the conference's decisions; the largest of these, the Primitive Methodists, used 'camp meetings' to put across a very simple message and chapels to bring together very simple believers. The tensions were increased by the dictatorial conservatism (including Toryism) of Jabez Bunting, president or secretary of the Wesleyan Methodist Conference for many years from the 1820s to the 1850s. During his time almost a quarter of the Methodists joined bodies not under his control. Only in 1907 did Methodism begin to reunite, when the Bible Christians, the Free Methodists and the New Connection buried differences which had become too hard to define.

By the 1890s all the 'Free' Churches, including all the Methodist groups, had so grown that their own numbers were keeping up with the population's and in total their regular supporters were almost as many as the Church of England's. But in comparison with the disciplined Roman Catholics and even with the argumentative Anglicans, they were handicapped by disunity, which brought at least one penalty: chapels were being built which were too many and too big, and the expense often burdened, with long-lasting debt, congregations whose numbers left the dismal impression that 'the church is empty'. The leaders had made the mistake of believing their own optimism, and the supply of seats with a good view of the pulpit vastly exceeded the demand for them.

In many places these chapels, now often called churches when they were not central halls, could attract considerable numbers to hear an unusually eloquent preacher or to enjoy what was offered as a 'pleasant Sunday afternoon' of recreation. But that formula for success belonged to a period which was beginning to be historic. The modern media of communication were arriving fast and the piety of the cottage was being bombarded. Modern leisure was also growing and it was no longer necessary to look to a church for entertainment. Modern transport was developing and on Sunday a bicycle or motor car did not have to be directed towards a church. Modern education was expanding – and spreading, sometimes very intentionally, the scepticism about the Churches' doctrines which had been cruder and less damaging in the unschooled generations. Life could, it seemed, be fun, and the Puritan morality which condemned alcohol, gambling, dancing and other pleasures could be ignored.

The first Englishman to popularize the term 'secular' in its full modern meaning (in 1851) was G.J. Holyoake, who in 1842 had been imprisoned for blasphemy. T.H. Huxley coined the less aggressive term 'agnostic' in 1869. Charles Bradlaugh formed the National Secular Society in 1866, and was allowed to take his seat in Parliament without taking a religious oath twenty years later. (A Jew had been admitted in 1858.) His admission to the House of Commons was a signal that the days had gone when Englishmen who had doubted or denied the existence of the Churches' God had felt it necessary to gather for warmth in little societies while the mental climate around them favoured Christianity. Now the Churches, even when taken together as probably they would not wish to be taken, could seem the minority. The educated writers who reached the public were seldom orthodox in religion; the half-educated in the new society were usually no more than half-Christian; and secularists began to publicize well-argued atheism through the Rationalist Press Association in 1899. In 1882 a parish priest who was also a theologian, F.J.A. Hort, warned a new Archbishop of Canterbury of the Church's 'calm and unobtrusive alienation in thought and spirit from the great silent multitude of Englishmen and again of alienation from fact and love of fact'. Queen Victoria continued to reign for almost twenty years after that alarm but the confident-sounding rhetoric of bishops and preachers was declaimed against the background which Hort had seen.

For most of the English the daily background was now urban or suburban life. During the nineteenth century the proportion living in cities with more than a hundred thousand inhabitants rose from about a tenth to almost 44 per cent. As we have seen, this move from country to town did not immediately mean a break with Christianity. The migration was at its peak in the 1820s and '30s, when the Anglicans disastrously failed to move with the people, but the people, or most of them, remained Christians in their own sense and might even attend a church, probably a Nonconformist chapel. Half a century later the Church of England was making a strenuous effort to reach the cities, where the Roman Catholic Church was already at work with great success and Nonconformists were becoming missionary. The most conspicuously aggressive mission was that of the Salvation Army, so named in 1878 by William Booth, formerly a preacher in a Methodist splinter group, now the dictatorial 'general' of a crusade which, like the Roman Catholic Church, eventually won great respect; but as the twentieth century opened every English city could be seen to be occupied by an army of Christians doing battle against sin and squalor. Yet it was profoundly significant that all these Christian groups tended to think in terms of a mission 'to' (rather than 'in') the cities, for year by year something vital quietly declined in the hearts and minds of the people who lived urban existences. This was the vivid belief in God as the Creator of nature and in Jesus as the Teacher of morals to a community. In the man-made city, nature seemed distant, there was no strong community and no desire for one, and many impressive voices could be heard which did not come from any pulpit. If people thought that they needed to be saved, usually it was from material poverty by political or other material means, not by religion.

And although in order to be realists we have concentrated on the social reality of religion – on the Churches as institutions or on the mostly churchless beliefs of the people – we should remember that the intellectual debate about the truth of Christianity had not been settled when in the 1760s 'Reason' had ceased to be the main challenge.

Now 'rationalism' appealed not merely to Reason as common sense but to detailed, known facts. Hort warned the archbishop about the danger to the Churches of the 'love of fact'. In the early years of the nineteenth century much was said or written by Christian believers in order to maintain the essential compatibility between 'Revelation' and 'Nature', but as the quantity of facts in reliable science increased the reliability of the Bible seemed far more questionable. For some years the crucial difficulty was in reconciling the accounts of the early years of the creation in the book Genesis (prominent at the Bible's beginning) with the facts being unearthed by geologists: fossils revealed an earth very much older than had been believed, and despite many claims no evidence was found of a universal flood. Then in *The Origin of the Species* (1859) and *The Descent of Man* (1871) Charles Darwin revealed a fact which seemed to be a substitute for the Bible's myths: the evolution of species through struggles to survive in an environment often unfriendly.

This fact could encourage 'Social Darwinism' by suggesting that ruthless capitalists (such as Cecil Rhodes whose wealth was derived from control of the trade in South African diamonds) were the fittest to survive in the jungle of the market place and that the 'Anglo-Saxon race' was fitted to rule the world (with Rhodes dreaming of a British dominion over Africa around a railway from the Cape to Cairo). As a scientist, Darwin was more cautious in drawing philosophical conclusions from his work but at least he demonstrated the descent of *homo sapiens* from other species, leaving in the minds of thoughtful Victorians a picture very different from the biblical picture of God making each species separately and perfectly for the enjoyment of Adam and Eve in the Garden of Eden. Then as the sciences of physics, chemistry and biology developed, many minds received the picture of a universe which – so far from being obviously designed by a benevolent Creator who then supplied miracles when needed – had come about through the accidental combinations of atoms or genes followed by the ruthlessly undeviating laws of material causation. Many Victorian scientists remained religious believers, perhaps making no real connection between religious emotion and scientific knowledge, perhaps with an interpretation of the Bible which acknowledged that it had no intention to teach science; to them, science was an activity blessed by God because it made possible an age of great progress. But for many, including much of the 'great silent multitude' with no direct access to science, the picture left was unfavourable to the kind of religion which having been 'revealed' had become organized and dogmatic. Progress, many people thought, would leave the Churches' God behind.

Even before the publication of Darwin's *Origin*, poets had articulated a mood of 'honest doubt', with some anxiety. Alfred Tennyson did so in *In Memoriam* and elsewhere: was death the final mockery of the pretentious hopes of Man? Matthew Arnold did so in *Dover Beach* and elsewhere: was the 'sea of faith' a tide which would never return? What moved contemporaries was the honest expression of doubt, as in Tennyson's

> I falter where I firmly trod,
> > And falling with my world of cares
> > Upon the world's great altar stairs
> That slope thro' darkness up to God.

> I stretch lame hands of faith, and grope
> > And gather dust and chaff, and call
> > To what I feel is Lord of all,
> And faintly trust the larger hope.

Other poets voiced a stronger faith: Robert Browning (a Nonconformist) in 'the grand Perhaps' which could be found by a great struggle; Christina Rossetti (an Anglican) in the Child to whom her heart was given 'in the bleak midwinter'; Gerard Manley Hopkins in the 'immortal diamond' since Christ 'was what I am', in a final salvation because already everywhere can be found 'the finger of God'. And Tennyson and Arnold finally adhered to some faith in the Eternal, inspiring and rewarding righteousness. But the great poetry of the age, with the struggle of faith and doubt as its central theme, had a tone very different from the confidence of many of the popular hymns. Whatever might be the faith which survived, it was a question of its survival because doubt or denial had challenged the assumption that God exists, loves and rules.

Darwin confessed that his long concentration on the hard work of science had diminished his attention to the spiritual side of life, and he showed that he appreciated the truth in the warning that Professor Sedgwick once gave him: if the picture of Man descended from apes through the 'survival of the fittest' in a world without spiritual meaning reached the public, 'humanity would suffer a damage that might brutalize it'. He subscribed to the funds of his parish church; he encouraged his wife and children to attend it; he was sometimes almost paralyzed by nervous disorders; in the end he was buried in Westminster Abbey. Yet he could not get out of his mind the thoughts which had destroyed the complacent religion of his youth, when he had vaguely intended to be ordained. The Old Testament was worthy of no more trust than should be given to 'the beliefs of any barbarian'. On the evidence no sane man should believe the New Testament's stories of miracles. No good man should admire without reservation a creation which included so much suffering, let alone a Creator who planned the everlasting punishment of hell. And although it was more difficult to relinquish all belief in God, 'can the mind of man, which has, as I fully believe, been developed from a mind as low as that possessed by the lowest animal, be trusted when it draws such grand conclusions?' And he knew that many shared such thoughts. In his old age he wrote: 'Nothing is more remarkable than the spread of scepticism or rationalism during the latter part of my life.'

Atheism or agnosticism spread far beyond the ranks of the post-Darwinian scientists. The year 1912 saw Thomas Hardy's deeply sad but definite poem about *God's Funeral*, and around this date many of the names of those who were beginning to have great cultural influence were not the names of men who defended traditional Christianity: to pick half a dozen, Forster, Housman, Lawrence, Russell, Shaw, Wells. Elgar did not remain the devout Catholic who had made great music out of Newman's *Dream of Gerontius*. But even so, the twentieth century would not have been so secular as it has been, had not seven days in 1914 included certain events.

On 1 August the Archbishop of Canterbury (Davidson) replied to an invitation for 1917: a celebration of the four hundredth anniversary of the Protestant Reformation was being planned in Germany. 'War between two great Christian nations of kindred race and sympathies,' he wrote, 'is, or ought to be, unthinkable.' His optimism seemed to be justified, since there seemed to be no sufficiently immense issue in dispute between nations which had felt close for many years (the Kaiser had held up the body of the dying Queen Victoria, who to the end adored the memory of her German husband). They had settled their disagreements over the colonial division of Africa. They had become rivals in commerce and naval power, but surely a great war would be madness of a kind that civilization had outgrown.

On 2 August the World Alliance for Promoting International Friendship through the Churches was formed at a conference in Switzerland.

On 4 August the British empire declared war on the German empire, which had invaded neutral Belgium. The invasion seemed necessary in order to get at France, which was allied with Russia. Germany was allied with the Austro-Hungarian empire which after provocation had invaded Serbia, Russia's ally which Russia felt obliged to defend. Britain was allied with France and Russia, so that Germany felt encircled. For some time the military chiefs in both alliances had been planning what to do in case of war, when large armies could be moved by the railways. Now plans had to be executed in order that the war should be over by Christmas.

On 7 August the editorial leader in the *British Weekly*, which had become the principal organ of Nonconformity and which might have rejected an imperialist and unnecessary war as a great evil, was headed: 'United We Stand'. The Anglicans and Roman Catholics were even more patriotic.

When conscription was introduced in Britain in 1916 'conscientious objectors' were exempted from combatant service, but in comparison with the numbers who volunteered or were conscripted the total was less than a third of one per cent. In the war, 772,785 men were killed in defence of 'King and Country' (or 'Empire'). Also dead was the belief that it was a definitely Christian nation: it was reckoned that less than a quarter of the army had been connected with any Church and although there were compulsory church parades only a handful turned up for a voluntary service. Yet men prayed before battle and were buried under crosses. What, then, was Christianity, down to the earth of the front lines? It was perhaps little more than a memory of peace and home with half a prayer to escape being killed. But also dead in most minds was the belief that the cross had been necessary in order to deter sentencing the whole of humanity to hell. Hell was real enough in the trenches in Flanders and France but the only profoundly Christian faith which could survive in it was, some thought, that the Father himself somehow suffers, so that the agony of the cross of Christ was the revelation of the Father's involvement in the pains of his children; suffers, and yet also judges, so that the war was the revelation of the consequences of Europe's sins. Many others, however, thought that the evil which had produced this slaughter inflicted by 'great Christian nations' on each other could never be explained or cured, and that the enigma surrounding this horror could never be pierced by any revelation or prayer. Humanity was indeed more brutal than the apes, and above the poison gas was a spiritually empty sky.

The English Churches were in some measure shielded from the fate of conventional religion at the front in the war. Among civilians prayers for safety and victory seemed no less than a proper contribution to the war effort, and the most influentially dismaying accounts of the soldiers' suffering did not reach the public before the late 1920s. On the whole the post-war atmosphere was one of an optimism restored: 'we have come through,' the right side had won, the League of Nations would make sure that the Great War had ended all war, England would be a home fit for heroes. And this mood was accompanied by a determination to punish the guilt of the Kaiser and his Germany by obtaining massive 'reparations' as vengeance; in the outcome, Germany was not allowed to rebuild itself in peace, and the peace treaty of Versailles was a prologue to a new European war. But there was some acknowledgement that lessons needed to be learned after 1918. The Church of England appointed 'committees of inquiry' which published a harsh account of the religious situation as disclosed by contacts between priests and people under wartime conditions. The clergy were 'out of touch with the thoughts and ideas of the time' and needed to be trained in science and in social and moral questions. The Established Church was regarded as 'the hereditary enemy of the working classes' – and with some justice, for 'some features of our industrial system' accepted by the Church could be compared with slavery. Cardinal Bourne felt that Roman Catholics had less need to be penitent: their priests had been closer to the men at the front, and capitalism at home had, he remarked, begun when the Church's property was stolen from it in the sixteenth century. But he did point out to his flock that the mood of the young soldiers who had survived the war was 'little short of revolutionary'. A Conservative, he had an eye on the Russian Revolution of 1917 and with good reason: the British Communist Party was to be formed in 1920 and there was to be a Labour government (however feeble) in 1924. And even if fears of a Red revolution in England were exaggerated, it was at least a fact that in 1918 almost every adult citizen – women as well as men – was at last allowed to vote in Parliamentary elections. After this concession the country could be accurately called a democracy, and bishops and preachers were not being foolish if they wondered whether in the future many people would accept their guidance.

Such seemed to be the outcome of the heroic efforts of the Victorian Churches to provide strong communities of faith. As Cardinal Newman looked back over his life in 1877, he confessed: 'I have all this time thought that a time of widespread infidelity was coming, and through all those years the waters have in fact been rising as a deluge. I look for a time, after my life, when only the tops of the mountains will be seen like islands in the waste of waters.'

6

Arrows of Desire

Post-war England, 1918–1997

After the First World War it became increasingly obvious that in England the Churches were not going to flourish on anything like the old scale. It was out of the question for any government to give a monopoly, or much other support, to any one Church or to all the Churches together, for governments were democratically elected and by the 1990s only about a tenth of the population was in regular contact with any Church. Church schools received State support since they provided a general education but there could be no guarantee that the teachers in them would be able (or in all cases willing) to persuade pupils to accept a Church's doctrines for a lifetime. Religious education and assemblies were included in the State's laws for its own schools but it was hard to make such laws effective and even harder to train children as believing Christians: most parents and teachers did not give that a high priority, some opposed it, and in some areas non-Christian religions were well represented among the pupils, even as a majority. Religious buildings remained a conspicuous part of the national heritage and as architecture might receive grants, but often the size of the congregation mocked the ambition of the building, and thousands of churches or chapels had to be used for other purposes, kept as empty monuments or demolished. Programmes about religion were included in the output of television and radio but for people who were interested (another number which declined) this could provide one more alternative to churchgoing. Churches were often used for weddings and funerals but even a church wedding often began a marriage which died because there was not a truly Christian attitude to it, and even a funeral conducted by a clergyman often ended a life lived without any great interest in the possibility of hell or heaven as traditionally conceived.

So did England become secular? Certainly the Christian religion became far more private, optional and problematic, not authorized by the State or public opinion but do-it-yourself. The contrast with most of the past was great – and so was the contrast with the attitudes of most of the two million Muslims, Hindus or Sikhs who settled in the urban areas as an unexpected epilogue to the imperial past. They used mosques or temples as community centres quite frequently, and mostly resented or ignored any criticism of their traditional faith although the younger members of this immigrant community could more easily accept the free-and-easy ways more typical of the English.

But if this was secularism it was of an English, inconsistent and tolerantly soft-centred variety. The modern or post-modern culture did not breed people as coldly rational as the computers which were in increasing use. Green or muddy fields near Glastonbury were filled with tents sheltering pilgrims to an annual festival of pop music. People still had emotions, imaginations, dreams and enthusiasms: young men were fanatically faithful in watching football; horoscopes were prominent in women's magazines; since life needed some excitement, drugs and gambling offered it; loving or difficult human relationships still fascinated human beings; and religion still added some colour to English life, perhaps in old traditions loved partly because they were old, perhaps in new movements and unconventional expressions, and perhaps encouraged by the post-modern rebellion against being 'modern' in a way which had been standardized and therefore was ultimately dull. As in William Blake's day there was hope for a 'New Age'. And the loyalty given to the Churches week by week was larger than that given to any other voluntary organization including the political parties. No confident philosophy with a moral content replaced Christianity; indeed, when the state of society was worrying, the Churches were quite often criticized for failing to give a moral lead with enough firmness, and paradoxically the critics could include non-churchgoers who like most of the public never actually listened to any preacher.

Although in some senses 'God's funeral' was proceeding as Thomas Hardy had expected, a closer inspection might reveal an empty tomb. Certainly few of the funerals of the English did without the Bible and prayer. Surveys of public opinion in the 1990s suggested that, of those who had coherent opinions, about a quarter of the population was either straightforwardly atheist or else convinced that although God might exist his existence could not be known. Very roughly another quarter believed in some 'higher power', and yet another in a 'personal' and active God despite many doubts. The last quarter consisted of believers in this God who were free of doubt although in some cases also free of the habit of churchgoing. Those who regarded themselves as definitely 'religious' or 'Christian' (whether or not they were regular churchgoers) could be expected to be female rather than male and older rather than younger, but belonging to a class did not seem to be decisive. The middle classes were more articulate but their opinions were divided, as were the opinions of those who were highly educated. The old feeling that the Churches were on the side of the bosses had died down, but so had any feeling that a normal working-class family had something to gain from contacts with a local church.

It is obviously very difficult to generalize about such a complex situation but it could be said that most of the English had an attitude to Christianity which was not aggressively hostile. It was influenced by the Christian centuries, so that even the irreligious could believe in Christianity as a 'way of life', now largely detached from Trinitarian orthodoxy and from the Churches as institutions or fellowships. Most people (even many believers in a 'personal' God) attended church only occasionally, for christenings, weddings or funerals or during the prolonged festivities of Christmas, but they were not unfavourable to the clergy, who gave them no trouble. They did not rely on miracles but a strong religious belief could be respected, even envied, as a source of psychological peace and strength, and among the many who found 'being religious' difficult or impossible 'being spiritual' was often very acceptable. Most people had few clear ideas about 'God' but did not believe that the word was quite empty of meaning. They had no desire to be thought saintly but they did reckon that they and other people ought to be modest, loving and tolerantly thoughtful in their personal relationships and ought to treat nature, specially animals, with respect. They did not believe that Jesus was either divine in the traditional sense or completely uninteresting; he had taught virtues of which they approved. They could find help in prayer or at least in a meditatively quiet time. This attitude might be called post-Christian but it was certainly different from the atmosphere in a definitely non-Christian society. England was not China.

At the end of the twentieth century the central problem for the Churches was how to keep warm in this cold climate, and how to keep open the possibility that they might become spiritual homes for more of the public. Instead of an agreed solution there was a far-reaching dispute about what to say, not merely how to say it. Many Christians were sure that a Church, however reduced in numbers and influence, ought to stick to the beliefs and moral standards taught by the Bible and handed on by earlier generations. Positive and energetic evangelism was thought to be necessary because the situation in society as a whole was regarded as grim. In the face of crime, violence, abortions, divorces and illegitimate births, and a general breakdown in morality and manners, the only cure could seem to be a return to the faith which had been forsaken. Essentially the same response had been made earlier in the century when the challenge had come from Nazism, Fascism elsewhere and Communism. The conservative Christians who made this response in the 1940s or half a century later were not necessarily wedded to all the details of the old faith or to all traditional ways of communicating it, but as a strategy what they desired was proclamation, not surrender. The Churches were therefore divided between liberals who wanted, and conservatives who resisted, more agreement with the public. Within these Churches there was one agreement in the 1990s that there should be what Blake called 'Arrows of desire'. To all it seemed right to pray for the modernization of the Churches; for their unity in the apostles' faith and mission; for wisdom in giving moral guidance in dilemmas which were often new; for a renewal of conviction about the truth of the essential faith. But there was little agreement about what was meant by such prayers. What was the right modernization or unity or ethics or faith? Which target was supremely important? The arrows of desire travelled in different directions.

* * *

The mood of idealism after the end of the Great War, and of confidence during the 1920s, affected the Church of England. A movement called 'Life and Liberty' believed (somewhat naïvely) that a reinvigorated life would be the result of liberty for elected representatives of the Church to form an opinion about its affairs in the parishes and dioceses and at the national level. By an Enabling Act in 1919 the Church Assembly was allowed to propose legislation about the Church's life which Parliament could approve or veto but not amend. Next year the bishops meeting in the international Lambeth Conference issued an appeal for Christian unity, insisting on the Bible, the sacraments, the historic creeds and the historic ministry of bishops (without demanding any single interpretation of it) but saying that they were willing to be 'commissioned' to minister in any other Church which shared their desire for 'reunion'. And in 1924 William Temple, the bishop who was to be the most influential Anglican leader over the next twenty years, presided over a conference on politics, economics and citizenship which without going into many controversial practicalities showed that many Anglicans now shared the 'little short of revolutionary' hopes for society which had been born amid the agonies of war.

Anticlimax followed. The creation of the Church Assembly did not result in any dramatic changes but the limits of the influence of the 'Catholic revival' within this Established National Church were exposed when the Anglo-Catholic leader, Charles Gore, resigned in protest against the decision not to restrict the parishes' new electoral rolls to confirmed communicants. Although the Church Assembly strongly supported a modest revision of the Prayer Book, mainly in order to accommodate moderate Anglo-Catholics, its proposals were twice vetoed by the House of Commons in response to Protestant fears during 1928–29, and what the bishops felt able to do was negative: they would not prosecute clergy who used the proposed new book. The appeal for Christian unity was not really followed up until 1946, when Archbishop Geoffrey Fisher proposed that, without any merger of institutions, 'intercommunion' with the Free Churches should be restored after the adoption by them of bishops ordained by Anglicans. On this basis, the Church of England could pursue the vision of 1920 but would not have to make any great sacrifice.

The 1924 vision of social justice was challenged in 1926 when a 'general', nation-wide strike was called after the demand of the owners of the coal mines that if international competition was to be survived wages must be lowered and the working week lengthened. William Temple and others who expressed sympathy with the miners did not protest very vigorously about their defeat, while the Archbishop of Canterbury (Randall Davidson, who during the war had protested against various examples of proposed ruthlessness) was not allowed to use the new instrument of the radio to broadcast an appeal for conciliation at the most critical moment. The reality was that, like the Established Church, the propertied class was not prepared to sacrifice its own interests. Davidson, a wise archbishop from 1903 to 1928, was no revolutionary, and Temple, who for a time belonged to the Labour Party, regarded it as his vocation to enlarge the Church's vision of a just society but saw the point of the protests which greeted any statement which seemed to be an excursion into party politics, unless the option being favoured in the pulpit was Conservative politics.

The Church of England's attention was naturally concentrated on its own life (it created five new dioceses in the 1920s) and on religious questions. The 1920s were the heyday of two movements which at least at their extremes were incompatible. The Anglo-Catholic Congresses rallied thousands of enthusiasts to an emphasis on the sacraments which in the 1930s was to develop into the Parish Communion movement, encouraging the full participation of the baptized (and confirmed) laity in a service which for Roman Catholics was still primarily an occasion for the priest to 'offer the sacrifice'. At the same time, however, modernist scholars were challenging the Church to revise its doctrines in the light of modern science and 'criticism' of the

Bible. The suggestions which they brought forward were not unlike the opinions of many of the laity who still regarded themselves as members of the National Church, but the more committed and articulate Anglicans, including the Anglo-Catholics, rejected them in favour of the traditional faith in a supernatural, miracle-working, saving God. It was into this faith that the modernist poet T.S. Eliot was baptized in 1927, coming out of what he saw as a 'waste land'. Another convert was C.S. Lewis, an Oxford scholar who was to have an influence larger than any preacher's in the presentation of a conservatively Christian vision of life, through broadcasts, popular books, novels and children's stories. When war returned, both men were to have considerable importance in the nation-wide feeling which made it a war fought in defence of 'Christian values' (the much used phrase).

Despite its internal tensions the Church of England still retained enough strength to be at, or near, the leading expressions of national unity and aspirations. In this period its own backbone was provided by its 'Liberal Catholics', who combined sacramentalism with a concern for human problems and an openness to modern thought. Temple could speak out of this central body of Church opinion and was also able to speak to a nation which needed its own unity. After the economic slump of 1929 (which weakened Germany's attempts to recover) a National Government was formed by a coalition of Conservatives with a part of Labour, led by the successive Prime Ministers, MacDonald and Baldwin. Mainly the coalition was supported by the south of England. That region recovered its prosperity fairly quickly, with prices falling and cinemas full, but as a whole the Church did show sympathy with the unemployed in the Midlands and the North: it was the first solid sign of a refusal to divide the nation into haves and have-nots. In 1936 came an even more novel sign of national unity, when almost all Anglicans accepted the impossibility of Edward VIII remaining on the throne when he insisted on marrying Mrs Simpson, an American with more than one ex-husband. The words 'family' and 'duty' were still potent and still had a Christian flavour.

Most Anglicans shared the general relief when Baldwin's successor, Chamberlain, claimed to have achieved 'peace with honour' by sacrificing Czechoslovakia to Hitler, and previously many had supported the Peace Pledge Union which in reaction against memories of the Great War advocated complete pacifism. But when the German invasion of Poland made the Second World War inescapable, Temple and other Church leaders gave a moral lead to national unity – and gave it in terms more Christian than the blind nationalism or imperialism of 1914. There was conviction that this very costly resistance to the aggression and atrocities of the Nazis was righteous, but there was also (at least sometimes) a refusal to endorse the morality of 'total' war, even when waged to destroy evil. George Bell, Bishop of Chichester, threw away his prospects of following Temple in Canterbury when he denounced the 'obliteration' bombing of German cities by the Royal Air Force. The great war leader Winston Churchill (a sceptic about religion) had no patience with such criticism. And during the war Temple, who died before its terrible final months, gave a moral lead, for example in a best-seller on *Christianity and Social Order*. Christians were well represented in thinking about post-war reconstruction, dealing with the social problems which had received no solution in the inter-war years. Amid the suffering and danger of a world war there was a mood of national unity and hope.

The Labour government elected in 1945 fulfilled many hopes of William Temple's brand of Christian Socialism. The problems of coal mining were eased for the time being by taking the mines out of private ownership. They were accompanied by the railways and by the water, electricity and gas industries. The Bank of England was also nationalized as a signal that the government intended to be in command of the economy. A contributory but State-supported system of National Insurance was established to finance the National Health Service, better pensions in old age and larger benefits to support the unemployment which, it was hoped, would become a rare misfortune. The Education Act of 1944 was implemented, providing a variety of State schools up to the age of fifteen, and meeting most of the costs of Church schools. The housing of the people was greatly improved. It seemed possible to maintain this 'welfare state' by taxing an economy which gradually recovered from the war. It was seen that Germany and its ally Japan, having been soundly defeated and devastated, were now thoroughly persuaded to devote their energies to the more profitable tasks of peace. The human and material cost of a war which might have attempted to preserve the British empire was avoided: the independence of India was granted in the 1940s, the independence of the African colonies in the 1960s. The Conservative Party was returned to power only on the understanding that it would respect and develop what Labour had achieved – which it did until the 1980s.

Some of the Labour leaders who achieved these steps towards justice in society were definitely Christian: the Prime Minister Clement Attlee was, as was Stafford Cripps. So, also, although in a reserved 'Church of England' style, was much of the post-Churchillian generation of Conservative leaders who provided an alternative administration within this agreed system. Such convictions and ideals contrasted with the atmosphere at the top of the national life before the 1940s and corresponded with a considerable recovery of Christian confidence in the nation at large. The Church of England derived some benefit from this new atmosphere. At last it gained the energy to modernize parts of its own life, reducing the number of independent parishes, ending the poverty in which many of its clergy had been living and also ending the absence of an up-to-date code of Church laws which many of them had rather enjoyed. Two archbishops, Fisher and Garbett, were conservative in many ways but did not hesitate to rebuke politicians when morality appeared to need authoritative declaration. In 1952 the coronation of Elizabeth II seemed also to be the celebration of a nation at peace with itself and with its conscience. Ten years later a new Coventry Cathedral was consecrated. Next to it stood the remains of the medieval church as a memorial to the devastation of the blitz in the war. It was built in the modern style, with art of high distinction contributed by Epstein, Sutherland and Piper. But essentially it was a traditional Anglican church: for example, the main or 'high' altar was indeed high and at one end of the building. It was not a church in which much attention had been paid to acoustics, to the problem of helping people to hear.

But in the 1960s the mood changed. Increased prosperity and education, and the decay of the class system, produced new freedoms, especially freedoms in criticizing 'the Establishment' and in enjoying the opportunities for sexual pleasure provided by the new availability of contraceptives. The energy of the new generation, both irreverent and optimistic, was voiced most loudly by the pop music amplified electronically, but the sound penetrated into the Established Church. Many took it as a cue for an exit: between 1960 and 1985 the Church lost about a third of its active membership. Most of those who left did so because they no longer needed any Church in order to be Christians in a non-traditional sense, but the departures could also be those of conservatives dismayed that the changes in the Church of England were as rapid as they were. They were not very rapid and were partly the management of decline, as in the arrangements for merger or teamwork between parishes which could no longer be staffed with the old lavishness. (Between 1900 and 1985 the number of clergy was halved while the population grew by two-thirds.) But there was also some creative innovation. Parliament was persuaded to allow the Church to authorize new forms of worship as an alternative to the Book of Common Prayer, and experiments took place. The Church itself allowed new forms of Christian teaching after the disturbance created by a paperback of a young bishop, *Honest to God* by John Robinson. God, he said, is 'the Beyond in the midst'; Jesus is 'the Man for others' and through this revelation of love the 'window into God'; prayer is life, not escape; love, not law, is the criterion of true morality. At last the contemporary world, or a radical and therefore selective interpretation of its hopes and needs, seemed to set the agenda. In part this could happen because the Archbishop of Canterbury was now Michael Ramsey, a man far more interested in theology and spirituality than in tidy administration, an Anglo-Catholic but one who fully accepted Newman's point that Catholicism must develop.

For a time there was talk about a radically new Reformation but it soon became clear that radical theologians were better at denying the relevance of old images and doctrinal systems than at reconstruction. Robinson himself set an example by returning to the reliability of the New Testament, which had indeed been his love before his exposure to the challenges of being a bishop in a largely unchurched London.

For the Church of England a large long-term effect was produced by a brief congress in 1967 when the Evangelical leader, John

Stott, set out persuasively a new strategy for that movement, which hitherto had retained from the old days of Calvinism a narrow concentration on the authority of the Bible, often taken without any complication, and on the aim of converting individuals to trust in Christ's death as the sacrifice accepted as a substitute for the punishment deserved for their sins. That had been the theology behind the preaching of American evangelist Billy Graham during the first of his visits to Britain, in 1954, which raised hopes of another 'awakening'. These doctrines were not abandoned but there was a new emphasis on loyal activity in the Church, on the weekly Eucharist, on the quest for Christian unity and on the responsibility to cope with social problems. In the years that followed Evangelicals also developed a fresh interpretation of the Bible, critically studying it as literature and history while still maintaining that it had been divinely inspired, and rephrasing its message ('taken as a whole') so as to be understood by modern people, particularly by the young. While in all these matters it could be said that the Evangelicals learned from those who were 'liberal' or 'radical', they also learned from Christians who were 'charismatic' with a simple new joy and an exuberant enthusiasm warming and lifting up many hearts. This extensive renewal of their tradition enabled them to become the dominant movement in the Church of England by the end of the 1980s, and to be prominent in making the 1990s a 'decade of evangelism' which put a brake on the numerical decline.

The purpose of this evangelism was to persuade people to move from half-belief in Christianity into commitment to Christ as Saviour within the community of the Church, but it was understandable if some of those invited knew enough about the Church of England to know that it was open to criticism as a community; that, indeed, it was eloquently criticized by its own members, although from contradictory points of view.

One outcome of the stirring of the 1960s was the conviction that the Church must be so organized that it could decide its own doctrine, worship and leadership, or at least have much more say in the decisions. This was granted by the State so that the Alternative Service Book of 1980 became possible and became widely accepted, in contrast with the fiasco of Prayer Book revision in the 1920s. In this new book little attention was paid to the radicals' challenges to traditional doctrines but the new services reflected the new self-understanding of the Church of England as a community of committed believers. The Eucharist was now clearly a celebration of Christ's self-sacrifice and victory by the whole congregation, not 'Holy Communion' for individuals; baptism was admission of a child or an adult to the Church as a new family; Christian marriage a solemn undertaking to live together in physical and emotional love sustained by God's own love, not a wedding which might have taken place in an office if the church had not been more romantic. But the expression of this commitment in understandable language did nothing to reverse the decline in the numbers being baptized or wed. In the sixty years 1930–90 the numbers in relation to live births for all marriages in the country declined from about 70 to less than 30 per cent.

It was also agreed that a committee representing the Church should submit two names to the Prime Minister when a diocesan bishopric fell vacant. The General Synod met for the first time in 1970; in this replacement of the Church Assembly bishops, clergy and laity had three 'houses' which could meet separately but which normally discussed together subjects drawn from the whole range of national and ecclesiastical affairs. The synod, in session two or three times a year, held many debates which could at least have an inspirational or educational value, the greater if careful reports had preceded them. It made many comparatively minor rearrangements in the Church's life, but possessed no effective executive body as a substitute for activity by the national government in earlier centuries. This kind of parliamentary system without a government was accepted until the Archbishops' Council was proposed at the end of the 1990s, together with a drastic slimming down of the General Synod and of the many meetings supporting it, which were expensive in time and money.

The debates in the Synod showed few sharp divisions reflecting party politics. This was surprising when in the late 1970s and throughout the 1980s Parliament was divided into, on the Left, a Labour Party so ardently Socialist that a minority left it to form a 'Social Democrat' group (later merged with the Liberals) and, on the

Right, a Conservative Party which under Margaret Thatcher became enthusiastic in the praise of capitalism as enterprising competition (which in the nineteenth century had been the economic creed of the Liberals). Majorities in the General Synod steadily rejected both extremes: for example, both the unilateral nuclear disarmament favoured by the Left and recommended in a report on *The Church and the Bomb*, and the dismantling by the Right of many parts of the nationalization-and-welfare structure of the late 1940s. As Archbishop of Canterbury throughout the 1980s Robert Runcie was perceived by many Tories (themselves no longer 'conservative' in a general sense) as a Shadow Leader of the Opposition: a remarkable role in view of the history of the Established Church. He commissioned a report on the social problems in the cities caused partly by the revival of unemployment in an economy swiftly losing its labour-intensive industries and not yet sustained by adequate training in technology. *Faith in the City* (1985) led to useful discussion and to practical projects.

But the divisions in the Church of England became very clear when the Church Assembly or the General Synod had to debate proposals to move towards reunion with other Churches. The British Council of Churches was formed in 1942, and by 1964 the experience of Anglicans and Free Churchmen working together in this fellowship had been so hopeful that a conference on 'faith and order' convened by the BCC dared to suggest that unity between the Churches could be achieved 'by Easter 1980'. Archbishop Fisher's initiative in 1946 eventually led to a detailed scheme – which, however, he attacked since it would involve an eventual merger with Methodism at the expense of the Church of England's unique position in the nation. The plan was also attacked because it involved, as 'stage one', a service of reconciliation between the ordained ministries. This could be interpreted as the 'conditional ordination' of the Methodist ministers by the Anglican bishops. Many Anglo-Catholics objected because this service would not be plainly an ordination by bishops in the 'apostolic succession', while many Evangelicals believed that even an act of this ambiguity was not needed: all that seemed essential to them was a common faith in the Gospel proclaimed in the Scriptures. Under these onslaughts the plan failed to attain the 75 per cent majority required, in 1969 and again in 1972. Ten years later a similar combination of opponents defeated a later plan to 'covenant' for unity, this time involving the United Reformed Church but not involving a service which could be interpreted as an ordination. Although most Anglicans were willing (rather than keen) to accept reunion with Methodism, and the Methodist Conference bravely produced adequate majorities in favour, many commented that the Church of England was itself so divided that it would never find it possible to agree on the terms of reunion with any other body.

Internal Anglican divisions surfaced again when the ordination of women as priests was proposed. Even in the 1960s this had seldom seemed a practical proposition and now the General Synod did not authorize the step until 1992. Many Anglo-Catholics argued that Anglicans had no authority to make such a radical change (whatever might have happened in the sixteenth century) and they were strengthened in their opposition by firm warnings from the Roman Catholic and Eastern Orthodox Churches. Many Evangelicals also objected or were hesitant because of teaching in the Scriptures about the 'headship' of the man over the woman. In addition there were objectors who were simply conservative or alarmed by the divisions. But whereas many Anglicans could feel in their hearts that the Free Churches were not worth uniting with at the expense of closer relationships with the Roman Catholics and Eastern Orthodox, at the end of the twentieth century it was harder to think that women never had vocations to the priesthood as genuine as those of men. The way had been paved by the earlier ordinations of women as deacons, to which many fewer objections had been raised from the Bible or the Church's tradition. One outcome was that three times as many women were made priests as there were male priests who resigned. Another was a new sensitivity to what might be implied by the constant use of exclusively male terms to refer either to God or to humanity. But yet another result was that some parishes refused to accept the ministry of women presiding at the Eucharist, or the ministry of bishops who ordained women as priests, and bishops who agreed with these dissenters had to be appointed to take care of them pastorally, in another striking departure from the Established Church's behaviour in the past.

It has seemed right to consider some of the nation's history in connection with the Church of England because despite the Church's numerical decline and internal divisions, Church and State continued to interact. Twenty-six of the bishops still belonged to the House of Lords; what bishops said could be noticed locally and even nationally; the General Synod and the committees reporting to it pondered many of the issues of the day; the clergy often took the lead in local Christian activities and felt free to approach anyone in the parish. In comparison, the Roman Catholic Church had only a small national organization and produced only a small commentary on current affairs – and then bishops usually spoke in exhortations and guidelines, apart from a clear and repeated condemnation of abortion. Like the Church of England it was now present all over the country and in every class, and it too had a large fringe of the baptized who were seldom seen in church, but it stood less chance of being regarded by the public as thoroughly English. It aroused both a greater respect (partly because some of the English remembered that almost a thousand million people alive around the world had been baptized as Roman Catholics) and a deeper dislike or fear (partly because few of the English forgot the history of censorship and persecution). Despite the strong elements of continuity with the Middle Ages, and despite its more modern heroes such as More, Challoner and Newman, it still had features which the insular English could only regard as foreign, in the shape of many imports of people and ideas from Ireland or from 'the Continent' or, at the highest level, from the English College in Rome, where future bishops were trained in almost total isolation from the vast majority of their fellow countrymen. Cardinal Godfrey, the most powerful Roman Catholic in England from 1938 to 1963 (first as Apostolic Delegate representing the pope, then as Archbishop of Westminster), had no intention of yielding an inch in the identification of Catholicism with Rome. Deliberately, the Church which he influenced was in England but not of England.

During the twentieth century the baptized Roman Catholic community in England grew from just under 1.5 to just under 4.5 million, and although most of the baptized did not attend Mass regularly it was remarkable that in the 1990s a million did. This was approximately the same as the number to be found in the Anglican church on an average Sunday and was a little more than a fiftieth of the total population. The higher proportion of committed supporters among the Roman Catholic baptized was a tribute to the work of priests, nuns and schoolteachers. In a subtler way it also resulted from the prestige gained for Catholicism by a galaxy of writers who in earlier years had presented it as the only viable alternative to the Godless philosophies which had brought spiritual, moral and material disasters to Europe. Some of these writers were clergy such as the witty Ronald Knox. Others were brilliant and widely read lay journalists such as G.K. Chesterton and Hilaire Belloc, who traced many modern diseases, social and psychological, back to the Protestant Reformation (to Belloc the 'English Accident'). Others were novelists including Evelyn Waugh and Graham Greene, voices from an unhappier time than the age of 'Chesterbelloc': Waugh a rude snob, Greene a womanizer, both on the edge of self-contempt and self-destruction, but both finding 'the power and the glory' in the Mass and by the very mixture and unhappy honesty in their characters both able to reach a public which was far from innocent.

The strength of this Catholicism, written about or lived, had little or no connection with political power although some of its laymen were influential in the media (which was one explanation of the growing disrespect for the Church of England in journalism). The strength lay partly in the message that the ultimate truths had been revealed, so that however urgent might be the need to confess personal sins there was no longer any need to ask ultimate questions; even the worst sins were assured of authoritative absolution through the Church. When Ronald Knox was asked by the bishops to make a new translation of the Bible the crown of his life's work, it was to be based on the Latin version not on the original languages. In 1950 when it was declared to be part of the Catholic faith that the Virgin Mary had been 'assumed into heaven body and soul' at the end of her earthly life, the doctrine was based on the Church's authority not on the New Testament. But the Church's strength also lay in the willingness to give answers to ultimate questions about human nature and human destiny; thus the glory of the Virgin Mary was seen as a promise to redeemed humanity. In this Catholicism could be heard unhesitating words which were now scarcely heard elsewhere: glory, horror, heaven, hell, holiness, evil, angels, devils, miracles, despair. At various levels of sophistication, from professors on their knees to old ladies on their deathbeds, these answers went to the heart. In a striking contrast with the reliance on 'Reason' without revelation or prayer which had been fashionable before 1760, these answers also seemed to be rationally defensible (experts could use the medieval philosophy of St Thomas Aquinas) – and it seemed that humanity, specially European humanity, could never rebuild a humane society except on the foundation of this estimate of Man as divinely created and divinely redeemed.

Furthermore, it seemed possible to convey this philosophy of life to future generations through Catholic schools, which in England were now well supported both by parents and by the State, and which were staffed by dedicated teachers. In these schools, it seemed, characters were trained. Whereas in the 1900s there had been an outcry against subsidies to Church schools, there was no noticeable opposition when the Education Act of 1967 increased the financial support or when the Act of 1988 tried to secure mainly Christian worship and teaching as part of the formation given in the State's own schools: such was the respect for the Roman Catholic (and, although to a lesser extent, the Anglican) contributions to the difficult task of building a spiritual and moral foundation for modern life.

Equally striking is the fact that this security inside a fortress-like community was shattered not by any lingering cry of 'No Popery!' or by the armies or the police of Hitler or Stalin but by the totally unexpected – and by him largely unexplained – decision of Pope John XXIII to summon the Second Vatican Council.

Already there had been some cracks in the wall of the fortress. In the Vatican of the 1930s the main policy was to come to terms with the dictators in the hope that Catholic worship and teaching would be allowed to do their quiet work unhindered, and the common bond of anti-Communism strengthened this hope. But when Mussolini invaded Ethiopia, or Franco destroyed democracy in Spain, or Hitler was seen in his true colours, this policy of the 'concordat' or alliance was seen to be as wrong as the politicians' policy of appeasement: a war had to be fought. Nevertheless, loyalty to Rome remained intense and it was seen that the papacy, being international, had to be neutral to some extent. During the war Cardinal Hinsley led the Sword of the Spirit movement to stress that it was fought in defence of Christian values. But in the 1960s Cardinal Heenan spoke for almost the whole of the community when he confessed to being bewildered by this unusual pope's decision to gather a bishops' council aiming at 'renewal', with 'observers' from other Churches. Since 1910 the number of Roman Catholic priests in England had risen from about four thousand to about six-and-a-half thousand. Should not the Church be praying for more priests who would teach the faith with assurance and care for the people with devotion? Why waste time on dangerous talk?

As reports came from the sessions in Rome, there was first astonishment at the chaos there; then elation, or in some cases great distress, that the assembled bishops had been inspired to 'open windows' to other Churches and to the modern world, frequently using words such as Scripture and truth, liberty and hope. The only new doctrine proclaimed was the teaching that everyone was entitled to freedom of religious belief.

The new era touched the average English congregation chiefly by the placing of the altar nearer to the people, the use of the English language and of preaching in the Mass, the encouragement of Bible study and the outburst of concern about the poor of the world (many of them also Catholics). But then came the blows. Many traditional Catholics hated the changes; many priests reverted to a lay status, partly in order to marry; many of the monks, friars and nuns grew confused about their vocations; many of the laity ceased to confess their sins to a priest; most pupils of Catholic schools refused to be permanently indoctrinated in orthodoxy although the moral influence often remained; most of the married couples refused to obey Pope Paul VI when he repeated the prohibition of artificial contraceptives; and then John Paul II led a conservative reaction to the disorder, delighting some, dismaying others. For a time it seemed that attendance at Mass and the numbers being ordained might at least hold up, responding to the optimistic spirit of the council. A Pastoral

Congress in Liverpool in 1980 demonstrated how many of the most lively people in the Church rejoiced that windows had been opened. But by the end of the 1970s it was evident that the total effect of the Council had not been to strengthen Church life in numerical terms, although good cases could be made for saying that it had improved its quality and had averted what would have been a worse decline without this injection of new life. Cardinal Heenan, who when younger had been full of bounce, died depressed. His successor, Cardinal Hume, being a Benedictine monk, took a calmer view but did not report a clear vision of the future.

The council had committed the Church to the ecumenical quest for Christian unity, in contrast to the 1920s, when conversations between a few Roman Catholics and Anglo-Catholics in Malines (near Brussels) had stirred up the indignation of the English bishops as well as of Protestants – and in contrast to the 1950s, when cold water had been poured over the work of the World and British Councils of Churches. It was natural that a pope should visit Britain for the first time in history (in 1982) and that there should be serious theological conversations between Roman Catholic and Anglican representatives. These produced agreements in areas which had been bitterly contested in the age of the Reformations. All could interpret 'justification' as the beginning of a process of 'salvation in the Church' which involved both a trust in Christ and a life appropriate to people grateful for Christ's saving work. All could interpret the Eucharist as more than a commemoration of the death of a Lord now absent: in that drama the Lord is present, really although not physically, and the remembrance by the faithful is the making effective in the present of an event in the past – the total event of Christ. Accordingly priesthood was seen as the presidency of the Eucharist and as the authority to convey God's forgiveness, banishing any suggestion of magic.

For a time it seemed that reunion might be possible on this basis. But here, too, there were anticlimaxes. John Paul II made it abundantly clear that he had not become pope in order to preside over the dissolution of Roman Catholicism understood as obedience to the teaching authority of himself as the successor of St Peter in harmony with the bishops appointed by him. Not even the diplomacy of the ecumenical theologians could produce a formula which satisfied both those who upheld and those who rejected this position. Indeed, by its decision to proceed with the ordination of women as priests the Church of England reasserted its independence against Rome, as it did by its refusal to take seriously objections to its continuing lack of independence from a single nation-state. At the end of the twentieth century there seemed to be no immediate possibility that Roman Catholicism would cease to look very Roman, at least at the top, or that this form of Anglicanism would cease to be really very English. The separation might prove permanent, but there were signs of hope, most prominently in the friendship between Liverpool's two cathedrals, the larger one built on a very grand scale between 1904 and 1978, the more modest Roman Catholic one a structure of concrete in the 1960s, with Hope Street between them.

What had come out clearly from the history of the century was that the main alternative to the Established Church, for the minority that was at all interested in church membership, was the Roman Catholic Church, not the Free Churches embodying the traditions of Dissent and Methodism. When the Roman Catholic bishops refused to join the British Council of Churches where Anglican and Free Church leaders collaborated, the decision was taken to replace that council by a less active one, which would be more acceptable.

Between 1930 and 1990 Methodist membership dipped from 727 to 416 thousand. It was a disappointment after the hopes surrounding the union of English Methodists in 1932, after negotiations since 1918. The United Reformed Church, formed in 1972 by a union of most of the Congregationalists with the small surviving Presbyterian body, halved its membership in the next quarter-century. If we seek an explanation of this sharp contrast with the expansion of the Victorian age, we shall not find it in any general refusal to accept the broad idea of nonconformity. On the contrary, the public at large insisted on its right to be religious in spirit, and even Christian in life, without conforming to these doctrines which were still taught jointly by the Anglican and Roman Catholic Churches – and also without conforming to the tradition of regular church attendance.

The true explanation seems to lie in the feeling of the English that if they were to take the trouble to belong to any congregation it would have to be one with an impressive centre, which in practice usually meant either the Bible or the Eucharist, or a combination of the two. Sermons, hymns and spontaneous prayers might still be attractive to the religiously-minded but they (or their equivalents) were now available through television, radio and reading. These things which had previously been the speciality of the Free Churches were also now offered by many Anglican and Roman Catholic churches, for there the old atmosphere of formality and uniformity had been blown away by the winds of the 1960s, and there seemed to be much less for Nonconformists to dissent from. In the Church of England in particular, freedom was not suppressed: the danger was, rather, that Anglicans might have become too free to be coherent. A mixture of education and fun could still attract some children but disaster overtook the Sunday School movement: primary schools improved greatly and the new institutions of children's TV, the leisurely weekend and the paid holiday lasting for weeks meant that parents no longer depended on Sunday afternoon for quiet or children on Sunday School excursions for excitement.

Many Free Church ministers read the signs of the times accurately and led their congregations to be more biblical and more eucharistic in emphasis, but they still faced the problem of how this position was to be distinguished from the position of other historic Churches with larger resources. If the Eucharist (or the Mass) was not wanted as the impressive centre of the congregation's life, the answer often seemed to be a firmly traditional attitude to the authority of the Scriptures coupled with a simple and happy acceptance of the authority of a confident preacher or other leader. In one rude word which was usually resented by those to whom it was applied, the answer to the problem of how to be successful might be 'fundamentalism' – which, on the whole, the historic Free Churches now rejected.

From the 1950s to the 1980s the leadership of the historic Free Churches put much of its energy into the ecumenical movement, collaborating and negotiating with the Church of England. It is possible that had the Church of England produced a warmer welcome these efforts might have resulted in a wide acceptance of reunion although there was always hesitation among Methodists and Congregationalists and it was very unlikely that the Baptists would be included: even if most of their congregations had agreed to accept the baptism of infants their attitude to the Bible was usually more conservative than had become normal in the Church of England and the other historic Free Churches. The failure of these hopes compelled a new generation of leaders to switch attention to a less ambitious project: the encouragement of smaller numbers in fewer churches, with local projects in ecumenical co-operation as a substitute for the collapsed national scheme. It remained to be seen whether these schemes could be revived now that the Church of England's Catholic element was divided and weakened after the ordination of women, and now that the worship in almost all the historic Churches was becoming similar to a degree which would have amazed all generations between the 1550s and the 1960s: the Eucharist at the centre with participation by the people, preaching from the Bible, an explosion of new hymns, the allowance of variety and informality instead of an insistence on uniformity. But although agreement about doctrines and convergence between practices might often be considerable, there seemed to be little excitement left at the end of the twentieth century about the possibility of a visible reunion. The historic Churches clung to their separate histories.

In the 1990s members of Churches formed since the sixteenth century were almost as numerous as either the committed Anglicans or the practising Roman Catholics, with the Methodists contributing about 400, the Baptists about 200 and the United Reformed Church about 100 thousand. But about 300,000 belonged to independent congregations which had been formed much more recently. Many of these were Christians who had migrated from the Caribbean and had not found that the colder atmosphere in the existing churches was favourable to their enthusiastic style of worship. Others were Pentecostal without being ethnic, belonging to a strong world-wide movement which celebrated experience of the direct power of the Holy Spirit. Other new congregations were 'house churches', seeing no need to meet in a consecrated building but certainly affirming the need to be consecrated in life according to the teaching of the Holy Scriptures as expounded by a trusted leader. What united them all was not any strong national organization but their own existence on a small, homely scale, offering the support which could not be offered by a churchless religion. If ecumenical dreams of a United Church were ever to be translated into reality, the reality was bound to include much diversity – but it seemed very unlikely that this new wave of Protestant Nonconformity could ever settle within any traditional institution. In its style of church life it had made a fresh start although it probably adhered to traditional beliefs about the Bible more firmly than did the historic Churches. Its aim could be expressed as the 'restoration' of the spirit of the New Testament while consigning the old institutions to history.

The twentieth century ended with those of the English who regarded themselves as Christians still divided, although without the hatreds and persecutions of the past. The divisions between the Churches were not insignificant since at least three million of the English still supported these institutions actively and further millions were attached to them more loosely, but the most basic divide was not between denominations. It was between those who did, and those who did not, believe that the expressions of Christianity should be adjusted so as to communicate more easily with an unchurched society. At the two chief festivals of the Christian year preachers were confronted by congregations which were almost bound to include some who were happy to take the great stories of the Bible literally, but which might well include others who were very sceptical about their historical value. Many preachers tried to solve this problem by emphasis on the devotional and moral aspects, not entering into much discussion of theology or of historicity: at Christmas 'Jesus can enter your life', at Easter 'Jesus is alive today'. But the division remained.

Understandings of 'mission' were different, as may be illustrated from the history of mainly Anglican efforts to be more involved in the life of the factory or office. In the aftermath of the First World War the Industrial Christian Fellowship was formed. It sponsored missioners who would speak to the workers with a definitely religious and definitely Christian message of hope, as the chaplains ('padres') had spoken to the troops before battle: sometimes the same men spoke in both settings. But after the Second World War 'Industrial Mission' usually meant that some specialist clergy would enable the laity in the workplaces to express their own insights, hoping for more collaboration between the management and the work-force, hoping too for a constructive approach to the challenge of competition. Both styles had the aim of enlarging the Kingdom of God, but they were very different.

In a similar spirit those who spoke for most of the Churches about ethical problems could change from being announcers of permanent commandments to being colleagues in the search for the least harmful consensus. In the 1920s most Churches accepted 'birth control' within marriage and in special circumstances. By the 1970s the circumstances did not need to be special, not even for most Roman Catholics. Indeed, the use of contraceptives was widely practised before marriage, and many Christians seemed to accept this development also. Abortion in certain circumstances was legalized in 1968; the change was accepted by most of the public although often with great reluctance, and by the 1990s more than 144,000 such operations were being performed legally each year in England. When divorce became an epidemic at first many Church leaders tried to hold the line that marriage was in principle indissoluble, so that in no circumstances could a church bless a second marriage while one of the previous partners was still alive. But as the State made divorce easier (beginning in 1937) there had to be a response from Christian pastors. In the Roman Catholic Church use was made of the possibility that the first marriage might be proved not to have been a true marriage. In the other Churches gradually some second marriages became acceptable to most consciences. Homosexual practice had traditionally been 'the love that dares not speak its name'; if between consenting adults it ceased to be a crime in 1967 and was often held to be natural in some and not a perversion. In this new climate gays and lesbians who made no secret of their sexual orientation, and did not preserve total secrecy about their practice, were increasingly accepted so that demands arose for public blessings on 'partnerships' in church and for full and open equality in the ordained ministry.

On issues not connected with sexuality there was a similar movement. Until the 1940s most Christians did not hesitate to say that there could be a just war and they would not be too shaken if it is pointed out that in practice this probably meant a war fought in defence of national interests; while others were convinced that no war could be compatible with the teaching of Jesus. But during the 1940s the realistic question became: what kind of force may Christians tolerate and even use in order to end or deter aggression? This question allowed a variety of answers – for many years answers which had to be given amid the prospect that the use of nuclear missiles would end most of civilization. Other unavoidable and very difficult questions concerned the application of ethics to economics. Most Christians, like most other people, ceased to believe either in restricted capitalism or in pure Socialism. The real moral question seemed therefore how to reconcile the energy of enterprise with care for the common good, and how to combine incentives for the enterprising with protection for the vulnerable, and it was a question about limits and balances in the 'social market'. For Britain, these problems about a swiftly changing society would probably have to be met within the European Union, where the future seemed to lie however hesitant the English might be about a single currency and a single government. In no sense was the mood crusading.

But morality still survived. The New Labour party led by Tony Blair won a spectacular electoral victory in 1997 by combining a very cautious economic policy (in effect abandoning Socialism) with an eloquent emphasis on social justice and personal morality. And as we have already noted, many Christians in the England of the 1990s gave a robustly old-fashioned answer to many of the questions asked by a modern or post-modern society. Any departure from what was treasured as the teaching of Scripture and Tradition seemed to be not maturity but treason; the insistence on complications seemed to be not sensitivity but a lack of conviction and confidence which was bound to result in a failure to communicate the Gospel. If the modern or post-modern English found the Gospel difficult to accept, so did the pagan Celts and the pagan Anglo-Saxons. What Christians had to do now was to stand firm. What the Churches needed was not criticism but support.

In the 1990s it was unclear whether these divisions within the churchgoing minority could ever be healed. The different Churches were closer than they had been in worship and friendship but each was still loved by some – and loved precisely because it was different. A number of translations of the Bible into contemporary language were used widely, with new hymns, but messages which could appear to be contradictory were derived from them. It was also unclear whether many of the English who were 'religious' and even 'Christian' but unchurched could ever be persuaded to take more interest in what was offered by any of the Churches, Anglican or Roman Catholic, Free or Independent. But at least to the hopeful it seemed possible that there might be more agreement between those who belonged to the Churches and some of the unchurched: an agreement to resist movements in thought and behaviour which would abandon the vision of God and of life's God-given dignity, and which would forget Jesus of Nazareth.

Whatever might be thought in 1997 about the rights and wrongs of English Christianity since 597, it could seem obvious that England would be poorer if in the future no life in this country were to end in the spirit of John Bunyan's Mr Valiant-for-Truth: 'I am going to my Father's, and tho' with great difficulty I am got hither, yet now I do not repent me of all the trouble I have been at to arrive where I am. My Sword I give to him who shall succeed me in my Pilgrimage, and my Courage and Skill to him that can get it. My marks and scars I carry with me, to be a witness for me, that I have fought His battles, who now will be my Rewarder'.

7

Mental Fight

The Next Century?

(The nature of this chapter is explained in the Preface.)

Unexpected events and movements occur in the history of Christians. The strength of Anglo-Saxon Christianity could not be predicted when Roman Britain was invaded by pagans. The almost total success of the medieval Church could not be predicted when the Anglo-Saxons were conquered by the Normans. The Protestant transformation of England could not be predicted at the beginning of the sixteenth century, nor the vigour of the Victorian Churches during most of the eighteenth. It is therefore possible that, in the future, groups or individuals from whom no great things were expected in the twentieth century will be honoured as the heralds of a renewal and revival which will (to use Blake's imagery) build more of 'Jerusalem' in England, in contrast with the story of decline and confusion which had to be told in the last chapter.

But in the 1990s there seems to be no reason to expect that the twenty-first Christian century will produce any very large increase in the numbers of the English going to church regularly. For the Churches, Blake's prayer is still topical: 'O clouds, unfold!'

Even the short and superficial account offered in this book may have suggested how many factors have contributed to the Churches' decline. Many more sources of companionship, pleasure and information have become accessible. Many more agencies, including the State and innumerable voluntary societies, have arisen to provide education and welfare and to advocate good causes. It was inevitable that the Churches should lose a prominence in society which still existed in the nineteenth century. Many new sources of knowledge have also become available to people seeking the truth about religion and about the human situation. It was not to be expected that the Churches, tied inescapably to Scriptures written in the ancient world and to their own long and rich tradition of theology and devotion, would find it easy to absorb the lessons taught by the new sciences. So it is hard to imagine any way in which the Churches, pushed by all these pressures, could have avoided a decline.

The Churches cannot escape all blame for their misfortunes. They have inherited a past which must to some extent now seem scandalous. When they were popular it was often because they represented not Christianity as defined by Christ but something very different: magic in obtaining fertility or other material benefits, or a respectability which might be complacent or hypocritical, or an insistence on the superior merits of a village, a nation or an empire. When they were powerful it was often because they were closely tied to a government and to local landlords or employers and therefore able to encourage the persecution of 'heretics' or 'dissenters'. Often they made little attempt to learn from the new knowledge, and often the efforts made to preach the Gospel as they still understood it to the new population in the industrial towns and cities were made too late and on too small a scale to tackle the problems effectively. Their own congregations were often not a very attractive advertisement for the Gospel of love, being all too human in their contempt for people belonging to a different religious or social group, and in their internal coldness or bickering. These and other failures by the Churches have been remembered and not forgiven.

Because the decline of the Churches has been so substantial and because their faults and failures have been so hard to deny, it seems likely that for most of the English what survives of Christianity will continue to be more or less churchless unless the Churches become radically different. It is of course conceivable that in a post-modern and post-industrial society attitudes will be much more favourable to the spiritual life and even to organized religion. There have been predictions that with work becoming less arduous, leisure or unemployment more plentiful and the consumption of the earth's resources more restricted, this combination of factors will persuade many people to concentrate more on activities which involve the use of time and mental effort, not of materials, and these activities will include religion. Indeed, there are already signs in the 1990s that people, especially young people, see the necessity of a lifestyle which does not depend on consumerism for its satisfactions. It has also been predicted that acute worries about society becoming brutal or more boring will drive many more people to a firm religion in order to counteract the spread of crime, the breakdown of family life, drug abuse and other evils – as some people have already been driven. But in the 1990s, these developments have not begun to bring people into the Churches on any large scale in England. A simpler lifestyle can be chosen without going to church and people can want to belong to a better society without belonging to a congregation.

Caution in expecting a revival of old-fashioned church life does not, however, mean that no strong survivals of the faith of fourteen hundred years will remain. On the contrary, it could be recorded in the last chapter of this history that in the 1990s belief in 'God' (however understood) was far more popular than atheism, and that many of the moral teachings of Christianity were still respected. It is evident that what Blake called 'the religion of Jesus', with the emphasis on 'Mercy, Pity, Peace, Love', has for many of the English outlived the religion of the Churches; and there seems to be no reason to expect any rapid change in this situation which is far from being completely secular or non-Christian, however disappointing it may be to loyal adherents of the historic Churches.

It also seems realistic to say that to an extent which differs from environment to environment and from person to person, the churchless version of Christianity is vulnerable. Some students of public opinion, including professional sociologists, interpret the situation positively as 'believing without belonging' but to others it is nothing more than an echo of the Churches' religion – and a dying echo at that. It is by no means clear that a firm belief and trust in the living God and a life-changing respect for Jesus will retain such strength as they now have if the decline of the Churches accelerates until it reaches the point where they have virtually disappeared. It is no accident that a history of Christianity must be so extensively a history of the Churches, since for most Christians the importance of a Church has been a part of the Christian message. From its beginning Christianity has been more than a philosophy: it has been a person and a community of people who have influenced their families, friends, neighbours and nations, more by what they have been than by what they have said.

A twentieth-century agnostic poet, Philip Larkin, wondered what people would think about church buildings if the beliefs which had been taught in them were to be forgotten completely. A church would still be reckoned 'a serious house on serious earth', he decided: in its emptiness it would still suggest the seriousness of human life and the possibility of being 'robed' in nobility. But it seems possible to say more than that about what these strange buildings have conveyed to people who use and love them, and about what they have to offer to those who pass by them in the street or who enter them very rarely. An appreciation of how Christianity made its biggest impact in the past will show what will be lost if churches, which used to be the centres of communities gathered for worship, become either museums or sites for developments regarded as progress.

It is natural that the surviving Churches should often be valued chiefly for what they continue to contribute to education, welfare and other good causes, or for their architecture or music, or for their hospitality to the lonely and distressed. These functions of the Churches can be admired quite easily without raising specifically religious questions. Indeed, even in the 1990s representatives of the Churches have earned respect, even among the largely unchurched English, for what they have contributed locally and nationally in these spheres. In 1996–97 two reports demonstrated that local activities could be inspired by a wide-ranging vision of a whole society more marked by justice and compassion: the 'social teaching' of the Roman Catholic bishops was summed up in *The Common Good*, and an ecumenical group went into more detail in *Unemployment and the Future of Work*. But in none of these spheres are the Churches unique. It seems reasonably certain that in the long run they will stand or fall according to the credibility of their statements and practices within the sphere of religion.

Religious feelings can arise out of the contemplation of nature, without any impact by a religion which claims to carry a special revelation of God. That was true about the pagans before Christianity arrived, about many of the country folk who went to the village church as part of life's routine, and about scientists and poets of a later age. It remains true about many who care for 'the environment' in the twentieth century. But the question whether the Force in nature cares for the individual comes to its climax through the fact of universal death. In the seventh century that point was made in the debate at the court of King Edwin. In the seventeenth century John Donne wrote, making three rhymes and two puns even at this extremity:

> I have a sinne of fear, that when I have spunne
> My last thred, I shall perish on the shore;
> But sweare by thy selfe, that at my death thy sonne
> Shall shine as he shines now, and heretofore;
> And having done that, Thou hast done,
> I feare no more.

And that light did shine from Christ's life and death for some amid the religious debates of the nineteenth century. Robert Browning saw it:

> So, the All-great were the All-loving too –
> So, through the thunder comes a human voice
> Saying, 'O heart I made, a heart beats here!
> Face My hands fashioned, see it in Myself.
> Thou hast no power, nor may'st conceive of Mine,
> But love I gave thee, with Myself to love,
> And thou must love Me who have died for thee.'

Moments of glimpsing eternity have occurred during many modern English lives but supremely they have come, for those prepared to have their eyes opened by the Scriptures and the sacraments of the Christian Church, through the experience of Christ which St Paul described as being crucified and raised with him. That encounter with Christ – that 'conversion' – has remained the heart of Christianity all through the changes of English history, and it can be expected to remain the heart. It is a heart which beats most clearly in the music or the words, the actions or the silence, when prayer is made within the Church as 'the fellowship of the Holy Spirit'.

The message did not begin in England: its origins lie very obviously in Galilee and Jerusalem. It reached Britain through this remote island's inclusion in the Roman empire and it returned through the mission to the Anglo-Saxons from Rome. Since then English Christianity has never been isolated and self-sufficient. Until the Protestant Reformation it was a part of Western Catholicism although it had its provincial peculiarities; then as the missionaries accompanied the traders, the soldiers and the settlers it became part of the expansion of the English language and culture across the oceans; then it began to return into the community of Europe. It can be expected that in the future it will take its place more fully in the religious life of the developing European Union. Despite all the difficulties involved, it can also be expected that Rome will be seen by many more Christians as the centre of Christian unity, never rivalled since a Roman army destroyed Jerusalem. What shape will be taken by the Roman element in the future of Catholicism cannot be predicted in the 1990s, when some see the Vatican as the world-wide Church's headquarters rightly exercising great powers while others want nothing to do with it. But it seems reasonably certain that the attempt of the sixteenth century to build up the Church of England as the one and only Church of the English people, established and favoured by the State but without any intimate fellowship with Catholicism elsewhere, will have to be abandoned sooner or later. The State does not now need the Church and the Church does not now need the State – at least, not on the old terms.

It also seems reasonably certain that attempts to impose uniformity on the English Christians belong to history, not to the future. No Church will be in a position to demand a monopoly or great privilege for its clergy and their teachings. No minority with strict standards of morality will be able to use the laws of the land to enforce the particular system of ethics which it upholds. Nor will any Church be able to impose uniformity on its own members. The Churches will have to find their own places in a society which is pluralist in its irreversible nature, and the leaders of the Churches will have to find their own roles in religious communities which share at least something of the general scepticism about leaders. The Churches will be free but in a free society; their leaders will be entitled to appeal to consciences but their members will persist in making their own decisions according to their own consciences.

During the twentieth century the division between 'conservatives' and 'liberals' in the Churches has become too deep for the gap to be filled by any action by any leader, however powerful or diplomatic. It seems reasonably certain that in England (as elsewhere) some will continue to respect the Scriptures in a way that is more conservative than the 'critical' way thought right by others; some will continue to find food for their souls in worship which is more traditional than the informal styles found helpful by others; some will be guided by moral laws regarded as permanent commandments and others more by consciences applying the law of love to situations which might be complicated. The personal factor will continue to count heavily as different temperaments react to different leaders and there will be contrasts between the genders, the generations, the social classes, the ethnic groups and the urban or rural communities. But whether or not the leadership wishes it, freedom will be exercised. Amid all these disagreements, what may unite will be neither dogma nor the denial of dogma. More unity could be found through the recognition that 'conservatives' can be helped by their tradition to be holy, and 'liberals' can be helped by recent discoveries to be truthful and realistic, both groups being disciples of Christ (the word 'disciple' means student). In that way mutual understanding would grow.

If we ask whether more agreement about the contents of the Christian faith will emerge out of this mutual understanding, there appear to be possibilities. It is not beyond realism to hope that Christians, 'conservative' or 'liberal', will be able to agree that Christianity cannot be Godless and retain its identity. This book has shown repeatedly that inspiration has come to English Christians from the belief that they had been allowed some contact with a source of 'grace' and strength more effective than anything that is visible. At the heart of this tradition has been trust in God, mysterious but real, eternal but present. Similarly, it may be agreed that Christianity depends on Christ, on the belief that 'God was in Christ' uniquely, on the experience that Christ still has the power to save from many evils. But some points more stressed by 'liberals' may also be agreed: that not everything in the Bible need now be taken literally (for strength in a religion is compatible with the use of the imagination to express awe-struck wonder), and that not everything in the Churches' traditions need now be taken legally (for what was the way of holiness for one generation may not be the best route for another). In his day Blake called England to 'Mental Fight'. He meant that the Gospel needed to be expressed in terms which would help the followers of Jesus to 'build Jerusalem' in what he saw as an evil time. He used the imagination of a poet and a prophet to speak about Jesus, who himself did not walk about Palestine laying down laws but instead proclaimed in the style of a poet, prophet or story-teller a vision of the Kingdom of the Father.

If we ask whether Christian unity will emerge out of more 'communion' between the Churches, we can say that it seems probable that the ecumenical movement which has been a novelty in the twentieth century will turn out to have been both a failure and a success. It is unlikely to achieve a complete union between many Churches in the near future, for experience has shown that plans to merge Churches can arouse passionate and prolonged opposition if they seem to destroy familiar and valued traditions. Enthusiasm for that kind of unity has been genuine for some notable Church leaders and for some minorities in church membership during the twentieth century, but it may well have been a reaction to the scandal of quarrels between Christians in a period when the world wars were raging or brewing and when secularization was a new phenomenon and therefore a new challenge to all religious believers. At the end of this century it appears probable that another kind of unity will prove to be a more achievable goal. In a gradual process, increasing contacts, friendships and co-operation between Christians in Churches previously separated may grow in 'communion'. In that process Churches are willing to recognize the essential faith, a faith using the Scriptures and sacraments, in each other, and they enrich themselves spiritually by learning from each other what has been valuable in the different developments of that faith. In this process there may develop agreements and unions which in the 1990s seem very difficult or impossible. Roman Catholicism may become more fully universal (the original meaning of 'Catholic'), moving further from positions taken in the western Middle Ages and from the authoritarian style developed in the age of the Reformations and in the nineteenth century. Evangelical and Pentecostal groups may become more open to what has been good in the modern age, moving further from the narrowness of fundamentalism. The divisions between the Anglican, Lutheran, Calvinist and Methodist traditions may be healed as the causes of those splits recede into history. Eventually even more Christians than at present may enjoy a communion with each other which is also a communion with the Bishop of Rome but which is, above all, a communion with the Christ who cannot be divided. It may be a sign of the future that in the late 1990s the Prime Minister is a firm Anglican married to a firm Roman Catholic although as yet they are not allowed to receive together the sacrament in the Holy Communion.

The mood of humility at the end of the twentieth century may be a good new beginning. It seems possible that if the English Churches were to be more fully international yet also local in non-essentials, more fully centred in Christ yet tolerant of many differences in interpreting, obeying and following him, and more united without being uniform, they would be understood, accepted and even joined by more of the English. They could be seen as the English 'Body of Christ' walking into what may be a very long future.

Further Reading

(in addition to books mentioned in the Preface)

BEDE

Ackroyd, Peter, *Blake* (1995)

Barlow, Frank, *The English Church 1000–66* (1961)

Barlow, Frank, *The English Church 1066–1154* (1979)

Bebbington, David, *The Nonconformist Conscience* (1982)

Bebbington, David, *Evangelicalism in Modern Britain* (1989)

Beck, G.A. (ed.), *The English Catholics 1850–1950* (1950)

Blair, Peter Hunter, *An Introduction to Anglo-Saxon England*, 3rd edn (1981)

Bossy, John, *The English Catholic Community 1570–1850* (1975)

Bruce, Steve, *Religion in Modern Britain* (1995)

Chadwick, Owen, *The Victorian Church*, 2 vols (1966-70)

Collinson, Patrick, *The Church in English Society 1559–1642* (1982)

Davie, Grace, *Religion in Britain since 1945* (1994)

Davies, Horton, *Worship and Theology in England, 1534–Present*, 3 vols (1996)

Dickinson, J.C., *The Later Middle Ages* (1979)

Duffy, Eamon, *The Stripping of the Altars: Traditional Religion in England 1400–1580* (1992)

Edwards, David L., *The Cathedrals of Britain* (1989)

Edwards, David L., *Leaders of the Church of England 1828–1978* (1978)

Fincham, Kenneth (ed.), *The Early Stuart Church* (1993)

Gilbert, A.D., *Religion and Society in Industrial England 1740–1914* (1976)

Gilbert, A.D., *The Making of Post-Christian Britain* (1980)

Haigh, Christopher, *English Reformations* (1993)

Harper-Bill, Christopher, *The Pre-Reformation Church in England* (1989)

Hastings, Adrian, *A History of English Christianity 1920–90* (1991)

Hornsby-Smith, Michael, *Roman Catholics in England* (1987)

Hornsby-Smith, Michael, *Roman Catholic Beliefs in England* (1991)

Kerr, Nigel (ed.), *John Betjeman's Guide to English Parish Churches* (1993)

Livingstone, E.A. (ed.), *The Oxford Dictionary of the Christian Church*, 3rd edn (1997)

Mayr-Harting, Henry, *The Coming of Christianity to Anglo-Saxon England*, 3rd edn (1991)

McLeod, Hugh, *Religion and Society in England 1850–1914* (1996)

Norman, Edward, *Church and Society in England 1770–1970* (1976)

Norman, Edward, *Roman Catholicism in England from the Reformation to the Second Vatican Council* (1986)

Parsons, Gerald (ed.), *Religion in Victorian Britain*, 4 vols (1988)

Rupp, Gordon, *Religion in England 1689–1791* (1986)

Spurr, John, *The Restoration Church in England* (1991)

Thomas, Charles, *Christianity in Roman Britain* (1981)

Thomas, Keith, *Religion and the Decline of Magic* (1971)

Watts, Michael, *The Dissenters: From the Reformation to the French Revolution* (1978)

Watts, Michael, *The Dissenters: The Expansion of Evangelical Nonconformity* (1995)

Welsby, Paul, *A History of the Church of England 1945–80* (1984)

Woolrych, Austin, *Commonwealth to Protectorate* (1982)

Index

French Revolution 105–6,
   110
Friends, Society of 3, 84–5
Fry 112
Funerals 139, 140, 141

Garbett 147
Gaul 6, 8, 13, 17
General Synod 150–3
Geneva Bible 69
George I 90; II 97; III 104
Gibbon 104
Gibson 99
Gildas 9
Gladstone 114–5
Glastonbury 2, 15, 27, 140
Glebe 27
Glorious Revolution 87, 89
Gloucester 47
God for Roman Britain 10;
   for 18th c. 94–7; for 19th
   c. 133–6; for 20th c. 137,
   141–2
Godfrey 153
Godwin 28
Gore 143
Gothic style 2, 104
Graham 149
Gray, R. 119; T. 98
Greene 154
Greensted 29
Gregory 18, 19, 26
Grey 62
Grindal 67

Handel 92
Hardy 135, 141
Harold 28–9
Hastings 29
Heenan 156–7
Hell 39, 137, 140
Henderson 128
Henry II 34; III 35, 38; IV
   41, 46; V 46–7; VI 46–7;
   VII 46–7; VIII 56–60,
   109; IX 88
Herbert 71–2
Hexham 21
High Church Anglicans
   118–20
High Commission 80
Hindus 140
Hinsley 156
Hinton St Mary 6, 12, 13
Hinton, W. 42
Hitler 146, 155

Hoadly 99
Hobbes 77
Holyoake 131
Homosexuality 162
Hooker 67–8
Hopkins 135
Horne 127
Hort 132–3
Host in Mass 44, 50, 60
House churches 160
Housman 136
Hügel 124
Hughes 126
Hume, Cardinal 157; D. 96–7
Huntingdon, Countess of
   102
Huxley 131
Hymns 101, 112, 160, 164
Hymns Ancient and Modern
   118

Illtud 9
Images 11, 50, 55, 62
Incumbents 99
India 101–2, 107, 111
Indulgences 43, 50
Industrial Christian
   Fellowship 161–2
Industrialization 3, 92, 104
Industrial Mission 162
Ine 15–16
Innocent III 37
Interdict 37
Iona 21
Ireland 33–4, 88, 107, 115,
   119, 121–2, 126

Jacobites 91
James VI and I 69–73; II
   82–3, 87
James the Deacon 20
Jarrow 6
Jerningham 123
Jesuits 64, 68, 123
Jewel 67
John 35, 37
John Paul II 156–8
Johnson 96
Joseph of Arimathea 1, 2
Josselin 81
Judicial Committee 117
Julian 42, 44
Julius 6
Julius Caesar 4, 6
Justification 157

Keble 119, 120
Kempe 44–5
Kent 17, 18, 20, 29
Keswick 117
Knox J. 63; R. 154

Labour Party 127–8, 138,
   146–7, 150
Lambert 59
Lambeth Conference 119,
   143
Lancaster, Duke of 45–6
Lanfranc 33–4, 36
Langland 42
Langton 37
Larkin 168
Latimer 53–4
Latinus 9
Laud 72–3, 76, 80
Law, W. 88
Lawrence 136
League of Nations 137
Lent 39
Leo XIII 123
Levellers 77
Lewis 145
Liberal Party 114, 128–9,
   151
Liberal theology 117, 144–5,
   161, 166, 171–2
Liberation Society 127
Lichfield 26
Life and Liberty 143
Lightfoot 118
Linacre 59
Lincoln 6
Lindisfarne 22, 25
Litany 59
Liverpool 121–4, 157–8
Livingstone 101
Locke 89
Lollards 41
London 6, 7, 19, 29, 38, 81,
   121
Louis XIV 83, 87
Lullingstone 6, 12
Lutherans 53, 57, 59, 61, 70,
   173
Lydney 5

MacDonald 145
Magic 11, 50
Magna Carta 35, 37
Mansuetus 9
Marlowe 65
Marriage 39, 44, 140, 150